THE MACE and the GAVEL

TRANSACTIONS

of the

American Philosophical Society

Held at Philadelphia For Promoting Useful Knowledge

VOLUME 87 · PART 4 · 1997

THE MACE
and the
GAVEL

Symbols of
Government in America

SILVIO A. BEDINI

AMERICAN PHILOSOPHICAL SOCIETY

INDEPENDENCE SQUARE · PHILADELPHIA

1997

Library of Congress Cataloging-in-Publication Data

Bedini, Silvio A.
   The mace and the gavel : symbols of government in America /
Silvio A. Bedini.
     p. cm. – (Transactions of the American Philosphical Society ;
v. 87, pt. 4)
   Includes bibliographical references and index.
   ISBN 0-87169-874-9 (pbk.)
   1. United States. Congress. House – Insignia – History.
2. Ceremonial maces – United States – History. 3. United States.
Congress. Senate – Insignia – History. 4. Gavels – United States –
History. I. Title. II. Series.
JK1319.B43 1997
328.73'07'0148 – DC21   97-30718
                                                    CIP

ISBN: 0-87169-874-9
USISSN: 0065-9746

TABLE OF CONTENTS

LIST OF ILLUSTRATIONS

ACKNOWLEDGMENTS

THE PREPARATION of this study, undertaken over a period of several years, has been made possible by assistance received from many, whose cooperation is gratefully acknowledged. Included are the late Julian P. Boyd; Lela Bodenlos and Claire Catron of the Smithsonian Institution Libraries; R. Breckenbridge Daughtrey, City Clerk of Norfolk, Va.; Mary Dessypris, The Library of Virginia; Mitchell G. Dorman, Sergeant-at-Arms, South Carolina House of Representatives; Martha Goodway, Conservation-Analytical Laboratory, Smithsonian Institution; John M. Jennings, Director, Virginia Historical Society; Louis H. Manarin, State Archivist, Virginia State Library; Cynthia Miller, Legislative Resources Center, House of Representatives; Richard Padgett, Sergeant at Arms, and Sandra K. McKinney, Clerk, South Carolina House of Representatives; Mary Monahan and Dee Orr, Office of the Speaker, Maryland House of Delegates; Edward C. Papenfuse, State Archivist, Maryland State Archives; Nancy O. Phelan, Commission on Arts and Antiquities, U.S. Senate; Edward M. Riley, Director of Research and Tracey Stecklein, Department of Collections, Colonial Williamsburg Foundation; Diane Skvarla, Curator, the Senate Historical Office; John K. Vandereedt, Archives I Reference Branch, National Archives Records Administration; Deborah Dependahl Waters, Curator, Museum of the City of New York; Barbara Wolanin, Curator, Office of the Architect of the Capitol; and my wife Gale. Also most helpful were the following, all now retired, Florian Thayne of the Office of the Architect of the Capitol; James Ketcham, Curator of the Senate; Richard Baker, Historian of the Senate; Kenneth Harding, Sergeant at Arms of the House of Representatives and Robert Hough, Assistant Sergeant at Arms of the Senate.

INTRODUCTION

WHEN the First Federal Congress convened in New York City, following the end of hostilities, one of the most urgent priorities of the newly formed legislative branch of the government of the United States, was formation of its organization. It is not surprising that it was formed of two bodies, similar to those of the British Parliament as reflected in the legislative bodies of the British colonies in North America. Next in order was the formulation of rules for the conduct of both of its chambers, and the selection of appropriate officials and devices to represent their authority. To execute the orders of the body, the need for the establishment of procedures for the maintenance of authority within the legislative bodies became immediately apparent. Following British practice once more, the new House of Representatives and the Senate appointed Sergeants-at-Arms.

A symbol of the body's authority was the next order of business. The House of Representatives adopted the mace, following the tradition of the mother country. The Senate instead used a gavel, in the form of an ivory knocker, to bring the body to order. Both of these symbols of authority have continued in use to the present time.

THE MACE
IN COLONIAL AMERICA

The ancient use of the mace introduces us to a remarkable instance of ecclesiastical casuistry. The clergy was forbidden to shed blood, and, as thus the sword was inhibited, this might have been thought sufficient to keep them from the battle-field. But not so; they adopted the mace; though they could not cut a man's throat, yet might they break his head. So Bishop Otho [Odo], half-brother of William, fought alongside the Conqueror at the bitter battle of Hastings with great effect. . . .

WILLIAM S. WALSH [1913][1]

IN RETROSPECT, it seems ironic that the symbol of the communality of the American people, chosen shortly after the achievement of their freedom, should assume the same form and tradition as one which for more than four centuries had signified the presence in the House of Commons of the oppressor of the American colonies, the British king! Originally a weapon for offense used primarily by cavalry for many centuries, the mace came to be universally regarded as a symbol of authority. It was modified in the Roman republic to represent the authority of its consuls, each of whom was attended in public by twelve lictors bearing an axe bound in a bundle of rods or *fasces*. This device symbolized the power assigned to the lictors under Roman rule to punish by flogging with the rods or beheading with the axe. The mace was introduced into the British Isles by Roman lictors attending magistrates holding office in the provinces of the Roman republic.

An early use of the device is represented in an eleventh century Bayeux tapestry depicting the Battle of Hastings, as the medieval bishop Odo of Bayeux, half brother of William of Normandy, is depicted riding into battle at the head of his Norman nobles holding a mace in his

---

[1] William S. Walsh, *A Handy Book of Curious Information*. Philadelphia: J. B. Lippincott Company, 1913. Odo of Bayeux (c. 1036–1097), was a notable warrior and statesman. A half-brother of William the Conqueror, he was the Norman bishop of the see of Bayeux and the English Earl of Kent. He fought at Senlac during the invasion of England. Despite his boundless ambitions and lax morals, he was a patron of learning, and may have commissioned the unidentified artist of the Bayeux Tapestry.

right hand instead of a sword, in order to conform to the canonical rule that forbade priests to shed blood. By the thirteenth century maces had lost their forbidding role, and were used for ceremonial as well as protective purposes established in France by the royal body-guard of King Philip Augustus and probably by Richard I in England, where it served more as a civic symbol than as a weapon.

When the Great Councils of the Norman and Plantagenet kings, who reigned in England from 1066 to 1327, gradually evolved into a Parliament which in the fourteenth century began to divide into two

FIGURE 1
Bishop Odo of Bayeux riding into battle with a mace.

Houses, the mace with fasces survived as the symbol of the English ruler. At first the House of Commons met only with the king's presence or approval. As the volume of government business intensified, however, and the House met with ever increasing frequency, the monarch's attention was absorbed more and more by court activities and official duties. It was no longer possible for him to attend all sessions. As a consequence, the practice was developed of sending his sword or mace to represent him. The symbol was conveyed onto the floor of the House with appropriate ceremony by the king's "Serjeants" to signify the royal presence and his approval of the meeting. A petition of the Commons in 1344 specified that only these designated representatives were deemed worthy to have maces made of costly metals.

Prior to the 1650s, it was the custom for each Serjeant at Arms in Ordinary of the Royal Household to have had his own mace, provided to him from the Jewel House by the Wardrobe, or later by the Lord Chamberlain. Upon the death or retirement of a Serjeant of the Commons, another of the Royal Serjeants at Arms in Ordinary was appointed to attend upon the Speaker, and he would be equipped with his own mace. This use of the mace in the House was interrupted only when the Long Parliament of 1653 was dissolved by Oliver Cromwell, who said, pointing to the mace, "Remove that fool's bauble!" which was promptly discarded. His objection actually was not to the mace itself, but to the presence of the symbols of the orb and cross. Accordingly, the Commons dispensed with all the elements that savored of royalty. Cromwell's instructions to the London silversmith Thomas Maundy, to whom he had granted the monopoly of making maces, was to substitute an acorn for the orb and cross on the new mace that the latter produced in 1649.

In about 1660, after restoration of the monarchy, the Maundy mace was redecorated and the royal symbols and insignia were restored. Made of silver gilt, the mace measures 4 feet 10½ inches in length, the shaft consisting of one short and two long sections, which are chased throughout with longitudinal branches from which spring roses and thistle flowers. The head is divided into four panels containing respectively a crowned rose, a thistle, a harp, and a fleur-de-lis. The royal crown with its orb and cross surmounts the whole, and includes the royal arms within the garter having lion and unicorn supporters; it features the motto *Dieu et Mon Droit* and the royal initials "C. R." for *Carolus Rex*. It is not hall-marked, and bears no inscription, date or maker's mark. The mace apparently spent a considerable part of its life in the Jewel House of the Tower of London or elsewhere, and was assigned to the House of Commons only in 1805, where it continues to be used to the present time, borne before the Speaker when the House is in session. Upon prorogation, when a session is postponed or terminated, the mace is removed from the House of Commons to the Lord Chamberlain's Office at St. James Palace, where it is kept until it is returned to the Serjeant before the opening of the Parliament.

By the beginning of the Tudor period, the ceremonial mace's customary blade-like flanges had evolved into arabesques of metal ribbon, and the bowl or head was engraved with the royal crest, causing the position in which the maces were held to be reversed. The earliest of the two maces of the House of Lords dates from the reign of William and Mary, 1689–1702. Maintained in the Jewel House of the Tower of London are eight historic massive silver maces of the Serjeants at Arms. Of particular historical interest is the mace of the Lord Mayor of London, for example, the mounts of the shafts of which are made of gold and crystal and set with pearls, and date from the medieval period, while the head was made in the fifteenth century.[2]

The authority of the mace of the House of Commons was challenged as recently as July 17, 1930. Protesting the House's action in suspending one of its members, John Beckett of the Labor Party seized the mace, declaring, "It is a damned disgrace!" and attempted to leave the chamber with it. He was intercepted by the Serjeant at Arms, however, who took the mace from him and replaced it on the Speaker's table. Beckett was suspended from the House.[3]

The mace served also as a common symbol of the British king's authority in his possessions overseas. Prior to the American Revolution several of the British Colonies in North America were provided with some form of the mace which they utilized in their legislatures—among them New York, Virginia, Maryland, North Carolina and South Carolina. It was often the practice in British seaport towns and admiralty courts to have their maces made in the shape of oars, a form adopted also in the British colonies of Massachusetts and New York,

---

[2] *Oxford English Dictionary.* 20 vols. and Supplement. 2nd edition (Oxford, Clarendon Press, 1989), vol. VI, pp. 4–5; *Encyclopedia Britannica.* 24 vols. (Chicago: Encyclopedia Britannica, Inc., 1943) vol. XVII, pp. 214–16; A. R. Browning, *The Mace* (Canberra, Australia: Australian Government Printing Office, 1970), pp. 1–4.

[3] John Hatsell, *Precedents of Proceedings in the House of Commons.* 2 vols. (London, 1818), vol. II, pp. 99, 140–44; Abraham Rees, *The Cyclopaedia, or Universal Dictionary of Arts, Sciences and Literature*, 39 vols. (London: For Longman, Hurst, Rees, Orme & Brown, 1819), vol. XXII, unpaginated, "Mace."

although no records relating to their parliamentary maces can be found in their State archives. Surviving, however, is the "mace" of the Vice-Admiralty Court of the Province of New York. Produced by the New York silversmith Charles LeRoux in about 1725, it is made of silver in the form of an oar 22 inches in length. One side is engraved with the British royal coat-of-arms, the title of the Vice-Admiralty Court, and an anchor and crown are inscribed on the reverse.[4]

The mace was employed as early as in the 1620s in the colony of Maryland as a symbol of resistance to the arbitrary rule of King Charles I, when the House of Commons sent forth its Serjeant at Arms with the mace to free one of its members imprisoned by the King's orders. Even George Calvert, the first Lord Baltimore, while serving as minister of the King, recognized the power of the House of Commons symbolized by the mace. When the King was attempting to stifle free speech and the right of petition in the House, Calvert had to answer for the King. He did his best to defend his master, but failed to persuade the House of Commons, the record noting the observation that the members ". . . could scarce believe" George Calvert ". . . and thinketh he equivocateth."

King Charles did not equivocate on the rights of the free-men, however, when the time came to grant a charter for the Province of Maryland. It was clearly stated in the charter that all free-men, or the greater part of them, or . . . their delegates or their deputies, were empowered to give their ". . . advice, assent and approbation" to any laws passed by the colony. The legislature lost no time, and in a few months insisted that not only did it have the right to agree to laws,

---

[4] The oar is on deposit in the Museum of the City of New York. Communication from Deborah Dependahl Waters, curator, September 16, 1988

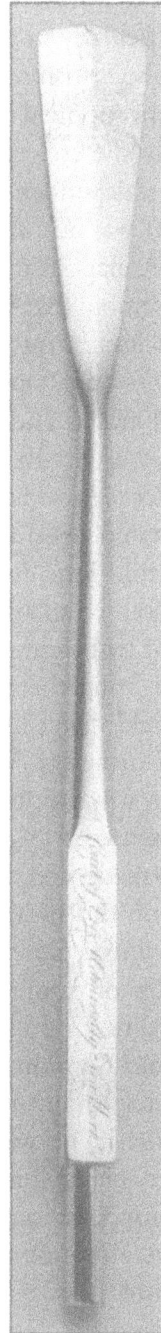

FIGURE 2
Silver Oar, mace of the
Vice Admiralty Court
of New York State.

but to initiate them as well, a concept with which Lord Baltimore was particularly in agreement. Thus it was that Maryland became the first of the British colonies in North America to have representative government specified in its charter as a fundamental principle, although it was only the collective action of all the colonies to achieve and maintain an independent nation.

It was not until Maryland's capital had moved from St. Mary's City to Annapolis in 1695, however, that the Lower House of the General Assembly (later designated the House of Delegates) was able to establish itself firmly as an independent voice in the colony's government. It was on its opening day on April 3, 1698 that ". . . After the Speaker had craved and received the assurances of the usual liberties of that House, His Excellency [Governor Francis Nicholson] was pleased to order a gown to be given to Mr. Speaker wherein he was immediately invested. Also the Governor gave to Mr. Speaker a small mace which he told him he might use and deliver to the person that should be appointed to attend this House, in the nature of a Sergeant att Armes, who by bearing the same, should have authority to take such persons and bring them before Mr. Speaker, as Mr. Speaker and the House should direct him."

During the 55th session of the House, on October 28 of the same year, it was noted, "At this time the mace, called also a staff, was again presented to the House. The Governor stated that the presentation was made, coupled with the proviso, that it be carried before the Chancellor, the Speaker of the House of Delegates, and Chief Justice of the provincial Court, the Commissary-General for Probate of Wills and Judge of Admiralty as occasion requires."

Almost immediately the House appointed a sergeant at arms, Daniel Cannon, to whom the mace was entrusted. In addition to enforcing order in the House and summoning witnesses to be brought before it, he was assigned other duties, including keeping the Town Gate, maintaining the town prison, and raising the flag over the State House. Cannon died shortly after his appointment, perhaps from overwork although it was not specified. Another sergeant at arms was appointed, but Anne, Cannon's widow, continued to raise the flag and to tend the Town Gate, for which she billed the Lower House.

The first recorded use of the mace in Maryland was in defiance of the Governor and his Council, when the House Speaker sent out the sergeant at arms to bring members of the Governor's Council back to the bar of the House. There they were asked to explain how they could ever have issued an order reducing the income of lawyers. Although their response is not clear, the issue appears to have been resolved in committee. The gifts of the Speaker's gown and the mace did little to keep the House compliant to the Governor's wishes, however. Whenever the Governor persisted in sitting in on the deliberations of the House, the Speaker found it convenient to become ill and the House adjourned with the mace to his chambers, which conveniently happened to be located in Rachel Proctor's Tavern.

Maryland's mace, which now consists only of an ebony rod 24½ inches in length and 1¾ inches in diameter, may have formed part of the original mace presented by the governor almost three centuries ago. It is capped on both ends with silver bands engraved with both sides of Maryland's Great Seal. The Seal was designed by Charles Willson Peale in 1794, executed on commission by the State, a seal that remained in use by the state from 1794 to 1817.[5]

The conveyance of a mace from Great Britain to the Commonwealth of Virginia, among the first of the British Colonies in North America to have received one, appears to have been first mentioned in an order of the English Privy Council of March 14, 1679. Noted on February 6, 1678/1679 in the *Minutes of a Committee of Trade and Plantations* was the statement that part of Lord Culpeper's proposals of December 14th ". . . is considered in reference to the impost of tobacco, presents to the Indian Princes, a mace & sword for Virginia & furniture for a chappell. . . ." The mace was not in fact sent at this time but on December 7, 1700, when Governor Francis Nicholson presented the House of Burgesses with ". . . a Gown to be worn by M.ʳ Speaker when you have elected and chosen such a one" in addition to ". . . a Staff or Mace to be borne before M.ʳ Speaker after he is confirmed by his Excellency (as an Ensigne and Token of Hon[o]ʳ and Power) . . . ." The House, which was then sitting in the Great Hall of the College of William and Mary, responded promptly to his Excellency with an address of thanks. The House then appointed John Chiles ". . . a Mace bearer and Messenger," who was subsequently referred to in the House *Journals* as its "Sergeant-at-Arms." In 1706 the House *Journals* recorded

[5] Elihu S. Riley, *A History of the General Assembly of Maryland, 1635–1904* (Baltimore, 1905), pp. 110, 115, 119; Edward C. Papenfuse, "The Speaker's Medallion," Address to Maryland House of Delegates, March 22, 1995; Edward C. Papenfuse, *"Doing Good for Posterity,"* (Annapolis: The Maryland State Archives and the Maryland Historical Trust, 1995), pp. 10–14.

FIGURE 3b
Detail of the head of the mace
of the Maryland House of Delegates.

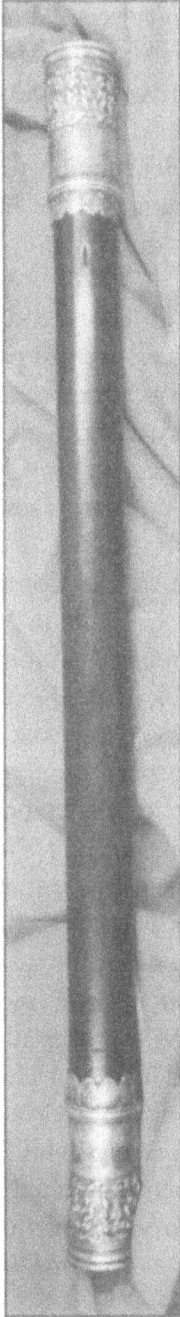

FIGURE 3a
The mace of the Maryland
House of Delegates, believed
to be seventeenth century.

A member of the house acquainted the house that the mace belonging to this house was broke, and moved that enquiry might be made, how it came by that disaster, and after a debate thereupon, it was moved, that the question be put, that enquiry be made how the mace came to be broken, which being opposed, the previous question was put, that the said question be put, and it passed in the negative.

Whether the mace was repaired at that time was not indicated in the records, but in 1722 an appropriation was made of £180 from the public money for various items to be purchased from England for the Capitol, among which were noted a new ". . . Mace, a Gown for the speaker, and a Gown for the Clerk of the House of Burgesses." No other mace was ordered thereafter, even following the fire of the Virginia Capitol in 1747, and apparently the 1722 mace was saved and continued in use. The next reference to the mace in the *Journals* was on February 1, 1727, when the House was organized and a Speaker was chosen. Then ". . . the mace was brought in and laid under the table." When the choice of Speaker was confirmed by the Governor, the mace was placed upon the table.

The *Journals* noted again in 1734 that at one point during the proceedings relating to the election of a speaker of the House, ". . . the mace was brought into the House and laid under the table, for the House was not deemed to be fully constituted until confirmation by the governor. In the House of Commons, however, the mace was laid at once on the table, and the speaker at once received his proper title and not that of speaker-elect." On August 16, 1736, Sir John Randolph was elected Speaker, and accompanied by the members of the House, proceeded to the Governor's mansion for confirmation. When they returned to their chamber, ". . . the mace was laid upon the table . . . ."[6]

On May 6, 1742 the House *Journals* noted that the mace was carried about the Capitol by the Sergeant at Arms and used to summon mem-

---

6 William Pitt Palmer, ed., *Calendar of Virginia State Papers and Other Manuscripts, 1652–1781* (Richmond: James E. Goode, 1875) vol. I, *Colonial, 1677–1680*, p. 341; *Journals of the House of Burgesses.* 6 vols. (Richmond: Virginia State Library, 1905–6), 1706, p. 196; *Journals of the House of Burgesses, Commons*, p. 393; *Journals of the House of Burgesses*, May 6, 1742; S. M. Pargellis, "The Procedure of the Virginia House of Burgesses," *William and Mary Quarterly Historical Magazine*, vol. 2, No. 2, April 1927, pp. 76–77, vol. VII, No. 3, July 1927, p. 153; Kenneth S. Harding, *The Mace. A History of the Mace and Its Use in the House of Representatives of the United States* (Washington, D.C.: Government Printing Office, 1972), pp. 4–5, 9.

bers to their places in the hall of the House and when bringing persons to the bar of the House for questioning. In 1756 Lieutenant Governor Robert Dinwiddie took the occasion to express to the House his resentment at ". . . the great indignity" offered the colony's Supreme Court by the mace-bearer, who had entered the bar and taken away such of the Court's ministers as were members of the House, an action without precedent.

Whenever the Speaker appeared in town in an official capacity, he was preceded by the Sergeant at Arms bearing the mace upon his shoulder. On June 1, 1774, for example, during the observance of the day of "Fasting, Humiliation, and Prayer" because of the closing of the port of Boston by the British, the Burgesses attended services in Bruton Church in a body, preceded by the Speaker who in turn followed the Sergeant at Arms bearing the mace.

Another mace was not ordered during the remainder of the colonial period, and it is probable that the mace purchased in 1722 survived the fire and continued to be used. Enough references to it occur in the House *Journals* to indicate that it was used constantly as in the House of Commons; before the election of each new Speaker it was placed under the table, and brought up upon the table when the House was in formal session and the Speaker was in the chair, and then placed under the table when the House formed "a committee of the whole" during which a committee chairman presided. The Sergeant-at-Arms also carried the symbol about the Capitol to summon members to their places in the hall of the House of Burgesses. The eventual disposition of the House of Burgesses mace is not known, for eighteenth century records of the City Council and Hustings Court are missing.

The City of Williamsburg, as distinct from the Virginia House of Burgesses, also had a mace of its own but how and when it was acquired is not known. It may have been ordered for Williamsburg by Governor Dinwiddie at about the time of his arrival in 1751, for it was similar to one he presented to the Corporation of Norfolk in 1753. The city mace was in use in Williamsburg during the period that the city served as the seat of government.

With the beginning of hostilities the mace apparently was concealed and kept hidden throughout the years of the American Revolution, and was brought to light once more after peace had been restored, and after the Assembly and state government had been transferred to Richmond in 1780. Thereafter the symbol was again displayed as occasion arose for local functions, and was featured again in the ceremonies held at Williamsburg to celebrate the proclamation of peace with Great Britain. The celebration, held on May 1st, 1783 included in fourth place in the order of the procession the ". . . Sergeant bearing the Mace" followed by the mayor, recorder, aldermen, common council and other officials.[7]

At some time after the American Revolution, the Williamsburg city mace was purchased by Colonel William Heth (1753–1808) of the Virginia Continental Line. He converted part of it into a standing cup ". . . of hospitable dimensions." It was inscribed with the colonial arms of Virginia and the mottoes: *En dal Virginia Quartam* [Lo, Virginia gives a Fourth (Crown to the British Sovereign)] of the Colony of Virginia, and *Virtute et labore florent Respublicae* [States flourish by Virtue and Toil] of the City of Williamsburg.

From about 1883 to 1911 the standing cup was on loan to the Virginia Historical Society, and in 1919 a member of the Heth family sold it to William Randolph Hearst. In 1939 it was purchased from the Hearst collection by Colonial Williamsburg, Inc. The mace was reconstructed from the original elements and regilded in 1941. A study of the designs confirmed that those on two sides were the crest, colonial arms and motto of the city of Williamsburg, and that the colonial arms of the Virginia Colony appeared on two others. The maker's mark revealed that it had been made by the London silversmiths Peter Archambo, Jr. and Peter Meure in about 1749–51, supporting the probability that it had been a gift to the city from Dinwiddie.[8]

As previously noted, in 1753 Dinwiddie also presented a mace to the Corporation of Norfolk. Fashioned of pure silver by the prominent London silversmith Fuller White in nine sections that screwed together, it measures 41 inches in length. Inscribed around the lower edge of the Norfolk mace are the words "The Gift of the Hon.[ble] Robert Dinwiddie

---

[7] Robert A. Brock, *The Official Records of Robert Dinwiddie, Lieutenant-Governor of the Colony of Virginia, 1751–1758.* 2 vols. (Richmond, Va.: Virginia Historical Society, 1883), vol. I, pp. xiv–xv; *Journals of the House of Burgesses,* vol. I, pp. 187–89; Dumas Malone, *Thomas Jefferson and His Time. Volume 1. Jefferson The Virginian* (Boston: Little Brown and Co., 1948), p. 131; "Peace Declared in Williamsburg, 1783," *William and Mary College Quarterly Historical Magazine,* 1st series, vol. XIV, April 1906, pp. 278–79.

[8] Rutherford Goodwin, *A Brief & True Report Concerning Williamsburg in Virginia* (Williamsburg, Va.: Colonial Williamsburg, Inc., 1959), 3rd edn., pp. 82–83; Elizabeth Dabney Coleman, "Ceremonial Symbol in Silver," *Virginia Cavalcade,* vol. 5, No. 3, pp. 39–42; John D. Davis, *English Silver at Williamsburg* (Williamsburg: The Colonial Williamsburg Foundation, 1966), pp. 239–41.

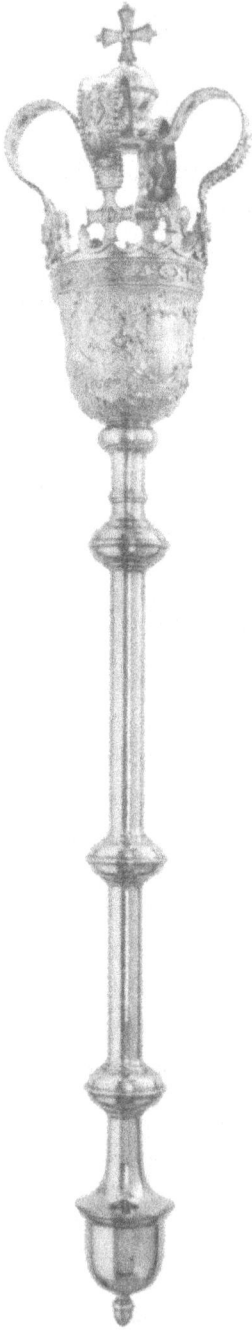

FIGURE 4a
Restored mace of
the City of Williamsburg.

FIGURE 4b
Standing cup that had been made
from the original Williamsburg mace.

Esq.ʳ Lieu.ᵗ Governour of Virginia to the Corporation of Norfolk, 1753." Among its decorations are panels with the emblems of England, Scotland, France and Ireland as well as the Royal Arms of Great Britain during the reign of King George II. Although completed by the silversmith in the year indicated, possibly because of delay in transit, it was not until April 1, 1754, however, that the Common Council was presented with the mace, and formally accepted the token.

The mace was kept hidden throughout the American Revolution, and used off and on during the next several decades in processions and at public ceremonies. This relic of royalty, ". . . the beautiful and bright, though ancient Silver Mace," was carried before the Mayor of Norfolk on September 15, 1836 in the procession parading its streets at the centennial anniversary of Norfolk's incorporation and borne again by Norfolk's municipal authorities on May 13, 1857 at Jamestown Island for the sesquicentennial celebration of the landing at Jamestown. In May 1862, when the city was being evacuated by the Confederates, the mayor became concerned for the safety of the relic. He removed the hearth stone in a room in his home on West Bute Street and carefully hid the mace beneath it. During the Civil War it appears to have been in the custody of the old Exchange Bank for a short period and was later kept in the Exchange National Bank, after which all trace of it was lost again for many years. Then, in July 1894, the Norfolk Chief of Police discovered the relic, in a state of great disrepair, hidden among litter and old records in a heap in a room at the police station. At the request of city officials, the Norfolk National Bank accepted its custodianship, undertook the necessary restoration and preservation.

On the first Armistice Day after World War I, the Norfolk mace was carried at the head of a triumphal procession, and its last public appearance occurred on August 16, 1932 in the procession commemorating the 250th anniversary of the founding of Norfolk. In 1952 the National Bank of Commerce of Norfolk paid to have two duplicates made of sterling silver, one of which was presented to the City Council to be used at public functions, and the other to the Norfolk Museum of Arts, while the original remains retired to museum status.[9]

---

[9] *Norfolk's Historical Mace*, pp. 5–16; "Norfolk's Historic Mace," *Arts in Virginia*, vol. I, No. 2, Winter 1961, pp. 20–21; *Norfolk's Historic Mace* (Norfolk: By Order of the City Council, N.D., pp. 5–16. Previously housed in the National Bank of Commerce in Norfolk, most recently it is in the Chrysler Museum in Norfolk.

In North Carolina the first mention of the appointment of a "Mace Bearer" and Sergeant at Arms appears in the colonial records in 1756. On October 16th a proposal made by Robert Jones at a meeting of the House of Assembly was approved, and it was ordered that Governor William Tryon accordingly be informed:

> This House taking into Consideration the necessity of a Mace Bearer beg leave to recommend to Your Excellency Daniel Dupree for that Office and desire that Your Excellency will be pleased to Commissionate accordingly.

No description of a mace has been found in North Carolina's colonial records nor in Tryon's papers, but Tryon approved the appointment of a Mace Bearer, and in the following year "An Account of the Ordinary and Extraordinary Expences, Civil and Military which are defrayed by Provincial Funds of the said Government 1767" noted that an appropriation was made for ". . . Mace Bearers & Sergeant at Arms to the Council £15 each."[10]

Among the earliest surviving colonial maces is the one belonging to South Carolina. The first State House in Charlestown, construction of which was begun in 1753, was first occupied three years later by the Governor, his Council and the Commons House of Assembly. On March 8, 1756, the Commons House of Assembly appointed a committee ". . . to provide Furniture for the Rooms to be appropriated for the use of this House in the State-House,

FIGURE 5
The mace presented to the city of Norfolk, Virginia in 1753.

---

[10] William L. Saunders, ed., *The Colonial Records of North Carolina*. 5 vols. (Raleigh: Josephus Daniels, 1887), vol. V, p. 714; William S. Powell, *The Correspondence of William Tryon and Other Selected Papers* (Raleigh, N.C.: Division of Archives and History, Department of Cultural Resources, 1980), vol. I, p. 448.

FIGURE 6b
Detail view of the crest
of the mace of the city of Norfolk.

FIGURE 6a
Closeup of upper section
of the mace of the city of Norfolk.

to send for a Mace, Robes for the Speaker, and a Gown for the Clerk."
A solid silver mace with gold burnishing was purchased in London at
a cost of 90 guineas.

Its form resembled that of the Maundy mace made for Cromwell's
Commonwealth government which was later embellished with royal
insignia. The Palmetto State's mace is engraved with the arms of the
House of Hanover and of the Province of South Carolina in addition
to Great Britain's royal arms. Scepter-like, it terminates in a symbolic

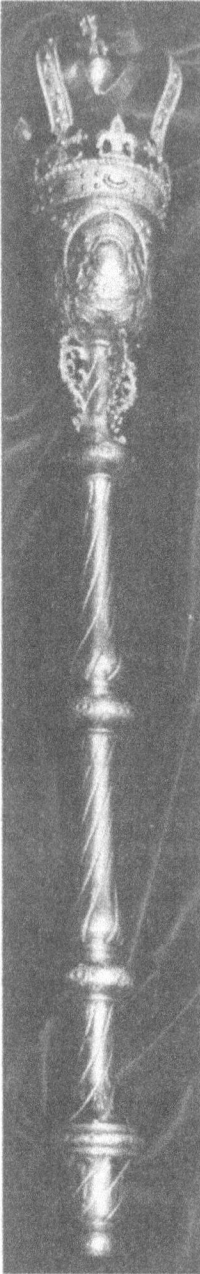

FIGURE 7
Mace of the House
of Representatives of
South Carolina, made
by Magdalen Feline
of London in 1756.

royal diadem modeled on the crown of St. Edward, with which English monarchs are crowned, adorned with repouseé representations of jewels, although no gems are included. Four circular decorative panels below the crown contain the obverse and reverse of the great seal deputed for South Carolina by King George II, an image of the king in full coronation regalia receiving the curtsey of a woman symbolizing South Carolina, and panels symbolizing agriculture and trade. The mace was made by a woman, Magdalen Feline, a member of the London guild of goldsmiths, who produced maces for several English communities. She first registered her maker's mark consisting of the initials "MF" at Goldsmiths' Hall on May 15, 1753 as a large-worker or specialist producing large pieces such as candlesticks, bowls, etc. Four other maces by Feline are presently known.

During the American Revolution South Carolina's mace was confiscated by Loyalist sympathizers who unsuccessfully attempted to sell it to the House of Assembly of the Bahamas Islands. In 1789 the House of Representatives voted to alter its design by the addition of republican symbols but no action was taken to achieve it. It was then deposited by Governor Thomas Pinckney in the Bank of the United States in Philadelphia. This action was known only to a few, however, and for many years the relic appeared to have been lost without a trace, until 1819 when Langdon Cheves, the Bank's president, found it and returned it to South Carolina, where it was deposited with the Secretary of State. The mace's ceremonial use was revived in the 1880s by Speaker of the House James Simons, Jr. The relic's adventures were not yet over, for in 1971 it was stolen, but law enforcement officers recovered it in Florida several weeks later. In 1978 the House of Representatives adopted a seal for its own use featuring the state seal with the mace superimposed across the front and the words "House

Representatives" and "South Carolina." The symbol of authority of
South Carolina's Senate is a Sword
of State.[11]

The maces of the American colonies apparently were constantly in use
up to the end of royal government in
America, and in some instances, continued thereafter. From entries in later
journals, in fact, it is apparent that
the mace of the Virginia House of
Burgesses continued being used for
some years after the establishment of
state government. Growing awareness
of the inconsistency of using a royal
symbol finally led to action resulting
in its abandonment. On December
10, 1792 a motion was made in the
House of Delegates that "*Whereas*, It
is inconsistant [sic] with the principles of a republican government, that
any badge or appendage of Kingly
pomp should remain therein," it was
". . . *Resolved*, Therefore, that the Executive be requested to procure two
maces for the use of the Senate and
the House of Delegates to be made
in such manner as they shall direct

FIGURE 8
Detail of the crest
of the South Carolina mace.

out of the materials of the one at present used." Bills requesting the
Executive to procure the two maces were passed by the House three
days later.[12]

In accordance with the instructions of the General Assembly, Gov-

---

[11] Sylvia W. Orange, ed. "South Carolina State Symbols and Emblems," excerpted from *The South Carolina Legislative Manual* (Columbia, S.C.: N.P., N.D.) unpaginated, "The Mace;" Alexander Samuel Salley, *The Mace, Bulletin No. 3* (Columbia, S.C.: Historical Commission of South Carolina, N.D.); Sandra McKinney, ed., *South Carolina Legislative Manual* (Columbia, S.C.: South Carolina House of Representatives, 1990); David C. R. Heiser, *South Carolina's Mace and Its Heritage* (Columbia, S.C.: South Carolina House of Representatives, 1991), pp. 1–11.

[12] Richmond, Virginia State Library, *Executive Letter Book, 1792–1794*, p. 290, letters from Henry Lee to the Speaker of the House of Delegates, December 10, 1792, October 21, 1793.

ernor Henry Lee immediately proceeded to commission two new maces to be made for the use of the Senate and of the House of Delegates. The first problem he encountered was the need for a suitable design for the symbol, which was to represent the Commonwealth's new statehood, and he turned for assistance to Thomas Jefferson, then Secretary of State. On May 16, 1793, Lee sent him a copy of the resolution of the General Assembly with a letter explaining, ". . . I very much wish to see fitly and ingeniously executed and feel a thorough sterility of genius on the subject. Nor have I been able to obtain aid here. Thus circumstanced I resort to your goodness and pray you will be pleased to favor me with a plan."[13]

Jefferson, gravely preoccupied at the moment with the arrival in Philadelphia of the French representative, Edmund Genet, turned for assistance to William Thornton, a self-taught architect with artistic talents who had won the competition for the design of the United States Capitol. Thornton readily rendered a design which he forwarded to Jefferson, with a letter noting ". . . In consequence of your inclination respecting the mace for Virginia I have drawn one which I submit to your superior Judgement." Thornton went on to make a plausible case for using the rattlesnake as a symbol, made all the more persuasive because of the use of the same device during the Revolution on the "Don't Tread on Me" flag.

"The rattlesnake," he claimed, "was peculiar to America, and although one of the most terrible of his tribe, is nevertheless endowed with qualities which make it a striking emblem of this Government, for it is peaceable, and strikes only in necessity, or self-defence. It does not, like other Animals, take advantage but gives due warning of Danger." He rejected the claims for the eagle, and might have added Franklin's famous observation that the bird was cowardly, rapacious, and frequently infested with lice, and therefore inappropriate for a national symbol. Thornton furthermore noted that ". . . the bald eagle was not peculiar to America, for it was known also in Russia, and by adopting it would imitate with servility the Device of several Courts of Europe—they took it from the Romans, most likely from the Persians, for according to Xenophon, they used the Eagle."[14]

---

[13] The Library of Congress, Manuscripts Division, *The Papers of Thomas Jefferson,* letter from Henry Lee to Jefferson, May 16, 1793; letter from Jefferson to Henry Lee, May 21, 1793.

[14] Richmond, Virginia State Archives, letter from William Thornton to Thomas Jefferson, June 8, 1793; communication to the writer from the late Julian P. Boyd, September 20, 1976.

Jefferson forwarded Thornton's design to Lee, advising that he would have responded much sooner by sending along the drawing he now enclosed, but that he had not been satisfied with the presence of the rattlesnake in the design. "There is in man as well as in brutes," he wrote, "an antipathy to the snake, which renders it a disgusting object wherever it is presented. I would myself rather adopt the Roman staves & axe, trite as it is; or perhaps a sword, sheathed in a roll of parchment, (that is to say, an imitation in metal of a roll of parchment), written over, in the raised Gothic letters of the law, with that part of the constitution which establishes the house of representatives, for that house, or the Senate, for the Senate, however if you have the same disgust for the snake, I am sure you will yourself imagine some better substitute; or perhaps you will find that disgust overbalanced by stronger considerations in favor of the emblem."[15]

Lee in the meantime had also consulted the civil engineer and geographer William

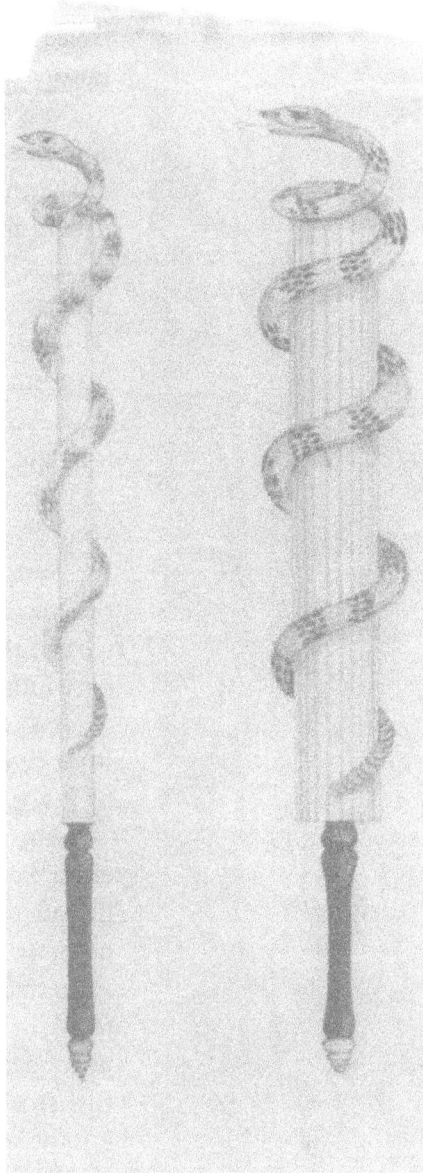

FIGURE 9
Drawing in water color by
William Thornton for a mace proposed
for the Virginia House of Delegates.

---

[15] The Library of Congress, Manuscripts Division, *The Papers of Thomas Jefferson*, letter from Jefferson to Governor Henry Lee, June 28, 1793, with sketches; Paul Leicester Ford, ed., *The Writings of Thomas Jefferson*. 10 vols. (New York: G. Putnam and Sons, 1895–1899), vol. VI, pp. 320–21.

FIGURE 10
Pen and ink sketch of
the design made by
William Tatham for
the mace proposed for the
Virginia House of Delegates.

Tatham, and the latter replied that he was averse to adopting anything already used in Europe because such might alarm the public, ". . . or a motto which may imply the abstract authority of separate jurisdiction . . ." and furthermore ". . . it would seem as if the American establishments were indebted to Foreign Powers for the capacity of Invention." Instead he proposed a design that included (1) a scepter as an emblem of the just Authority of The People when legally represented; (2) a Globe supported thereon, exhibiting the American Coast and Atlantic Ocean, ". . . thereby intimating that her sacred Rights and blessings are open to every being under the Sun;" (3) a Dove–". . . of the species peculiar to America perched on the Virginia part of the Globe . . . ;" (4) ". . . an Olive entwining the scepter of authority; and (5) ". . . a Crotalus horridus–coil'd round the Root of our Authority and the Sacred Tree of Peace."[16]

Tatham subsequently reported to Governor Lee stating that as Lee had requested he had met Waddel and Richardson to whom he presented the mace design. It had been suggested that either the material of the old mace, or the funds proceeding from its sale, be used for the new maces. It was agreed that Richardson was to proceed with the work but the latter had cautioned him that it would be a project greater and more costly than had been expected by the Legislature.[17]

In October Lee submitted the designs produced by Thornton and Tatham to the General Assembly with a letter to the Speaker

---

[16] Richmond, Virginia State Archives, letter from William Tatham to Governor Lee, July 21, 1793.

[17] Richmond, Virginia State Archives, letter from William Tatham to Lee, July 23, 1793.

of the House of Delegates stating "A disappointment in the expectations of having the same executed [has] rendered it impractical to provide them in time for the present session." In the following month the House passed a resolution directing that the Executive be requested to sell the mace ". . . now used by this house and that the proceeds of the sale be deposited in the public Treasury." The resolution applied not to a new mace but to the old colonial mace inherited from the House of Burgesses.[18]

On December 3, 1794 the auditor's office reported that the old mace ". . . weighing one hundred and one ounces at 6s p'r Oz . . . ." had been sold by the Executive for one hundred one dollars to William and George Richardson, partners of a prosperous silversmith firm, and that the proceeds were to be paid to the Treasury. No further entries relating to new maces appear in the records of the period and in all probability they were never produced after all. In 1962 the Virginia General Assembly received a new mace from the Jamestown Foundation that had been purchased in England.[19]

---

[18] Richmond, Virginia State Library, *Executive Letter Book 1792–1794*, p. 290, letter from Henry Lee to the Speaker of the House of Delegates, October 21, 1793; Palmer, ed., *Calendar of Virginia State Papers*, vol. VII, p. 371, Resolution of November 17, 1794; "The Mace of the Virginia House of Burgesses," *Virginia Magazine of History and Biography*, vol. XIX, July 1911, pp. 305–306.

[19] Palmer, ed., *Calendar of State Papers*, vol. VII, p. 191, Report of the auditor's office, December 3, 1794, vol. VII, p. 371, House resolution of November 17, 1794, vol. VII, p. 391, December 3 1794, sale of mace to William and George Richardson; "The Mace of the Virginia House of Burgesses," *Virginia Magazine of History and Biography*, vol. XIX, July 1911, pp. 305–6.

THE MACE
OF THE UNITED STATES
HOUSE OF REPRESENTATIVES

The House is a sanctuary, a citadel of law, of order, and of liberty; and it is here—it is here, in this exalted refuge here, if anywhere, will resistance be made to the storms of political phrensy and the silent arts of corruption; and if the Constitution be destined ever to perish by the sacrilegious hands of the demagogue or the usurper, which God avert, its expiring agonies will be witnessed on this floor.

AARON BURR [MARCH 2, 1805][20]

ON APRIL 14th, 1789, exactly one week after the Senate had appointed its Doorkeeper, a resolution was adopted by the House of Representatives, specifying that

A Sergeant at Arms shall be appointed, to hold his office during the pleasure of the House, whose duty it shall be to attend the House during its sitting, to execute the commands of the House from time to time, and all such process, issued by authority thereof, as shall be directed to him by the Speaker. A proper symbol of office shall be provided for the Sergeant at Arms, of such form and device as the Speaker shall direct, which shall be borne by the Sergeant when in the execution of his office.[21]

The first to be appointed to the position was Joseph Wheaton of Rhode Island, on May 12th, and he served throughout the first ten Congresses, until October 27, 1807. The "proper symbol" for the House selected by the first Speaker, Frederick Augustus Conrad Muhlenberg of Pennsylvania, was a mace. He had no precedent for reference, but the mace seemed to be the obvious choice, inasmuch as it had been used in similar circumstances in several British Colonies in North America prior to the American Revolution.[22]

---

[20] Aaron Burr, March 2, 1805. U.S. Senate, *Annals of Congress*, 8th Congress, 2nd session, p. 71.

[21] House of Representatives, 1st Congress, 1st session; Harding, *op. cit.*, p. 1. L. Carson Hampton, "The First Congress of the United States," *The Pennsylvania Magazine of History and Biography*, vol. xiii, no. 2, 1889, pp. 129–52.

[22] Harding, p. 9. Joseph Wheaton (–1828) of Rhode Island was elected by the House

Undoubtedly Frederick Muhlenberg and his fellow solons of the House of Representatives selected the mace as the House's symbol in 1789 simply because of their awareness of its existence in the legislative bodies of the several royal colonies. It is possible that Muhlenberg turned to Maryland for a model, as the first mace was described as consisting of a bundle of ebony rods wrapped by a silver band from the center of which rose a single rod capped with an eagle in silver. It is doubtful, however, that they were fully aware of the symbol's origins nor of its significance and the implications of its use when they ordered that one be made.

During the early discussion in the House on the selection of a mace as its symbol, there was some indecision concerning the manner in which it was to be used. It was suggested that it remain on the Clerk's table during sessions and that it be placed under the table when the House was in Committee, following the practice of the British House of Commons. The suggestion was rejected, however, at the session of the House held on April 7, 1789, when the body voted on the adoption of the House rules.[23]

A description of the first mace has not survived, but based upon the appearances of its later replacements it featured the Roman fasces and an American eagle with widespread wings as its dominant themes. The identity of the New York silversmith commissioned to produce it was not recorded. A likely possibility is that it may have been Myer Myers, whose shop in 1789 was situated near Federal Hall. Myers, who was Chairman of the Gold and Silver Smiths' Society, produced many rare forms of American silver not attempted by other silversmiths of the period, including a number of pairs of *rimonim*, or Sefer scroll bells which were somewhat similar in form to the mace.[24]

The House's mace was first instituted when the Congress met in New York City and it moved with the Congress to Philadelphia and later to Washington. It was customary after the President had delivered his annual message to the Congress, now known as the State of the

---

of Representatives on May 12, 1789. Although his father and brothers were Loyalists and commissioned British officers, he joined the Continental Army in 1775 and was wounded in action. He served as Sergeant at Arms until October 26, 1807. He later served with distinction as a colonel in the War of 1812 and his death in 1828 was attributed to a saber wound to his head received in the American Revolution.

[23] *Our Capitol, Senate Document 50* (Washington: Government Printing Office, 1966), pp. 28–29, 43–45; Harding, pp. 2–3.

[24] Jeanette W. Rosenbaum, "Myer Myers, Early New York Goldsmith," *Antiques*, vol. LXV, No. 2, February 1954, pp. 124–27, 154; Graham Hood, *American Silver: A History of Style, 1650–1900* (New York: Praeger Publishers, 1971), pp. 126–32.

Union message, for the House to select a committee to formulate a reply, and the Senate followed a similar procedure. After the reply had been approved by the full House, the House members formed a procession led by the Sergeant at Arms carrying the mace to the President's residence where the Speaker delivered the address. Among the earliest records of this procedure was an account of the event occurring on December 13, 1790,

> At two o'clock, the House, preceded by the Sergeant-at-Arms, waited on the President of the United States, at his house, where the Speaker delivered the following Address in answer to his speech to both Houses.[25]

Ever since the use of the mace was first instituted in the House, each day that the body is in session, it is called to order by the Sergeant at Arms or the Deputy Sergeant at Arms. Entering the chamber bearing the mace before him he places it upon a cylindrical pedestal provided for it at the right side of the Speaker's chair. The pedestal is made of polished green marble rising forty-four and one-half inches from the floor. The mace is supported upon its base by means of a rod projecting through its center that fits into an opening in the marble. The symbol remains in this position during the entire period that the legislative body is in session. When the House resolves itself into Committee of the Whole House on the State of the Union, the Sergeant at Arms moves the mace to a lower pedestal provided for it beside his desk, so that it is readily apparent whether the House is in session or in Committee. When the House is adjourned or in recess, the mace is kept in the office of the Sergeant at Arms upon a white marble base.[26]

The mace has had to be used with relative infrequency in past years to bring order among turbulent members of the House. During confrontations that occurred from time to time over the years, order was always restored by presentation of the mace, the authority of which has never been disputed. Although no formal record of its use has been maintained in official records, it was noted again and again in the press and by popular writers of the time. If or when a House member becomes offensive or beyond the Speaker's control, the Speaker orders the Sergeant at Arms to proceed. The latter removes the mace from

---

[25] Joan Sayers Brown, "The Mace: A Proper Symbol of Office," *The Washington Star*, June 5, 1977, p. 23; Harding, p. 15.

[26] Asher C. Hinds, *Hinds' Precedents of the House of Representatives of the United States.* 11 vols. (Washington: Government Printing Office, 1907–1941), vol. 2, section 1346; *Our Capitol*, p. 45; Harding, pp. 2–3.

its pedestal and approaches the offending Congressman, presenting the mace before him. This action almost invariably has the desired effect of causing the offender to pause, and peace is restored once more in the chamber.

The first encounter requiring the use of the mace by Joseph Wheaton, the first Sergeant at Arms of the House, was to resolve a brawl that took place in Congress Hall in Philadelphia on January 30, 1798, during the 3rd session of the Fifth Congress, between Matthew Lyon of Vermont and Roger Griswold of Connecticut, which led to a resolution to expel Lyon. The encounter was illustrated in a contemporary engraving entitled "Congressional Pugilists" as the two Congressmen faced each other. Identified also are Speaker Jonathan Dayton, the Clerk of the House Jonathan Condy and the Chaplain the Reverend Ashbel Green, all apparently amused. The Sergeant at Arms there beside the Speaker's chair, is not shown with his mace. The engraving featured also a bit of doggerel:

> He in a trice struck Lyon thrice
> Upon his head, enraged Sir,
> Who seized the tongs to ease his wrongs,
> And Griswold thus engag'd, Sir.[27]

An early mention of the use of the mace occurs in an account of the second session of the 6th Congress, held on November 22, 1800, the last under the Federal administration and the first to be held in the city of Washington. President John Adams had driven in his carriage from the President's House across Tiber Creek to read his message to the Congress which opened the session. He delivered an eloquent speech that was well received by both houses assembled in the Senate chamber. As noted, usage required that the House would respond to the President at the Presidential mansion in a personal attendance of the whole House. A committee appointed for the purpose chaired by Roger Griswold prepared a reply, but then a problem arose—how would it be possible for the entire membership of one hundred and six members of the House to travel to the President's House, given the conditions of the roads?

Among those attending was Congressman John Cotton Smith (D) of New York, who later reported the event. ". . . the only access [to

---

[27] Harding, pp. 5–8; Browning, passim. Illustration from the Barber Conable Collection, Office of the Architect of the Capitol.

FIGURE 11
"The Congressional Pugilists." Contemporary engraving illustrating
the encounter between Roger Griswold and Matthew Lyon
in Congressional Hall, Philadelphia, February 15, 1798.

the President's House]," he stated, "was by a road [Pennsylvania Avenue] long and circuitous to avoid the swamp already mentioned, and the mud very deep. Fortunately a recruit of hackney-coaches from Baltimore, by their seasonable arrival, enabled us to proceed in fine style, preceded by the sergeant-at-arms with the mace, on horseback. We were received with great courtesy; the answer was well read by the speaker, the members all standing, and the reply of the president truly appropriate. After partaking of refreshments, the House returned to the Capitol in the same order. Thus ended the last official and personal interview between a president of the United States and either branch of the national legislature." The ceremony was the last of its type to be delivered because President Thomas Jefferson discontinued the practice of delivering the annual message in person, a practice not resumed until the presidency of Woodrow Wilson.[28]

The original mace continued in use until it was destroyed by the British when they burned the Capitol building in the sacking of Wash-

---

[28] Rev. William W. Andrews, ed. *The Correspondence and Miscellanies of the Hon. John Cotton Smith* (New York: Harper and Brothers), 1847, p. 208.

FIGURE 12
Congress Hall in the U.S. Capitol as it appeared between 1821 and 1822.
Painting in oils on canvas by Samuel F. B. Morse.

ington on August 24, 1814. To maintain the now established tradition, a replacement was promptly ordered to be made of ordinary pine and painted, having the same general form and design of the original. It was to serve until such a time as it became convenient to order a new one. The wooden substitute was used for twenty-eight years. In October 1841 House Speaker John White ordered a new mace from William Adams, a reputable silversmith in New York City.[29]

In his commission to Adams, Speaker John White specified "You are authorized to have made a *Mace*, similar to the *one* destroyed by fire in the year 1814—for the use of the House of Representatives." It is

---

[29] William Armstrong, *The Aristocracy of New York: Who They Are, and What They Were; Being a Social and Business History of the City For Many Years. By an Old Resident* (New York: New York Publishing Co., 1848), pp. 10, 12. William Adams (fl. 1829–1862), a native of Troy, N.Y., was listed as a silversmith in New York City directories from 1829 until 1862 with a shop at 185 Church Street operated with steam power. In addition to his craft, he acquired great wealth from real estate investments. In 1842 he was elected president of Aldermen (Fifth Ward) and in 1850 and again in 1852 was appointed Commissioner of Repairs and Supplies. The selection of Adams to produce the House mace may have been largely a function of his political activism.

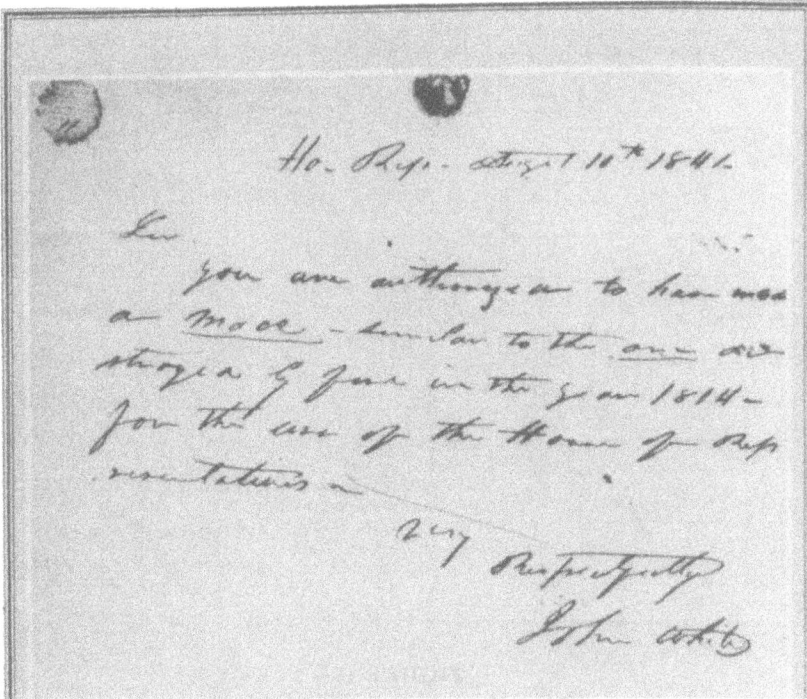

FIGURE 13
Order from Speaker John White commissioning William Adams
to have a new mace made in 1841.

not recorded whether a sketch or list of specifications were provided
to Adams, and it is interesting to speculate whether a description or
sketch of the original was available, or whether it was described to him
verbally. Adams completed the assignment in the following year and
the House records noted payment made for it from the "Contingent
fund for the period from December 1, 1841 to December 1, 1842,"
in an undated entry for ". . . William Adams, a mace for hall H. R.
. . . $400.00." On December 30, 1842 Adams signed a receipt for pay-
ment received for ". . . Making a Silver Mace surmounted with a Globe
and Spread Eagle."[30]

---

[30] National Archives and Records Administration, Group 217, Department of the Trea-
sury, *Records of the Accounting Officers, Treasury Account 86181, Voucher 4,* "Statement of the
Expenditure of the Contingent Fund of the House of Representatives of the United States
from December 1, 1841, to December 1, 1842 . . .," 27th Congress, 3rd session, Document
No. 10. Serial volume 418, page No. 2, of Document 10; Joan Sayers Brown, "William
Adams and the Mace of the United States House of Representatives," *Antiques*, vol. CVIII,
No. 1, July 1975, pp. 76–77 and cover illus.

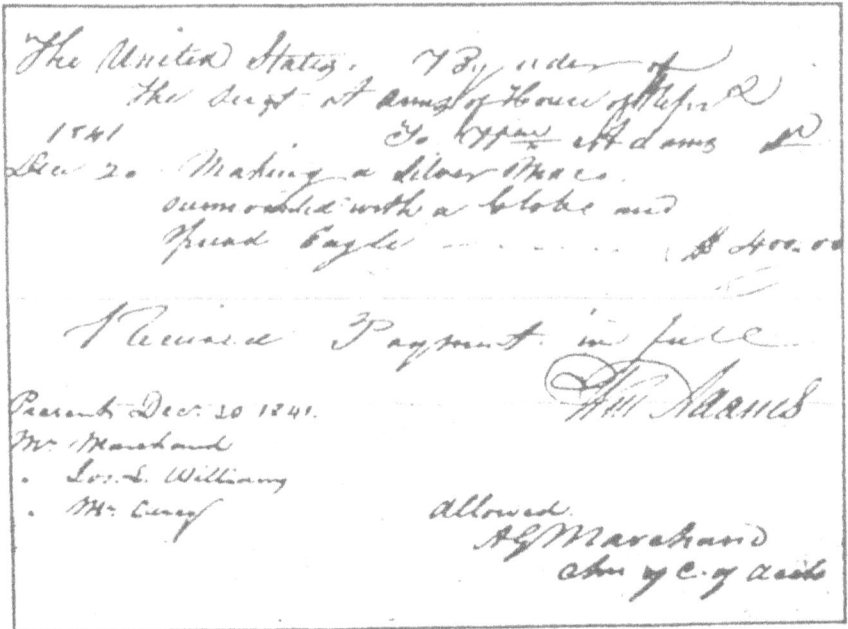

FIGURE 14
Receipted invoice from William Adams
to the House of Representatives, December 20, 1841.

Measuring 46 inches in height, the mace is made of coin silver and
consists of 13 individual cylindrical rods of ebony bound around a
central shaft, originally made of wood now replaced with bronze. The
rods are held together top and bottom by engraved silver bands 2¼ and
2½ inches in diameter respectively. Four crossing strips of silver are
wound helically around the shaft from top to bottom. The shaft terminates in a hollow silver globe, the surface of which is engraved with
the seven continents and the meridians of longitude. A silver eagle
with outspread wings surmounts the globe at the position of the
North Pole, upon a band marked with the degrees of latitude. The
name of the maker, place and date—*Wm. Adams / Manufacturer / New
York / 1841*—are engraved upon an escutcheon on the silver band
around the base of the mace.

The new mace was first used by the House on December 29, 1842,
during the 2nd session of the 27th Congress. As reported by the *Congressional Globe*,

The new Mace, "with silver clasp'd and with silver bound"—the sign and
token of the dignity of the House of Representatives—appeared, was qual-

ified, and took its station (in the room of the Sergeant at Arms). It is the work of 'William Adams, 185 Church street, New York.'[31]

During the two decades preceding the Civil War, tensions between the North and the South were escalating and it became increasingly difficult to organize each new Congress and elect officers. One of the most memorable incidents, however, noted in Benjamin Perley Poore's *Reminiscences,* occurred on December 3, 1849, during the 31st Congress, relating to the election in 1847 of Robert C. Winthrop of Massachusetts as Speaker. No party held a clear majority, and a preceding acrimonious debate on the subject of slavery was participated in by Representatives Robert Toombs (D) of Georgia, William Duer of New York, Thomas Henry Bayly (D) and Richard Kidder Meade (D), both of Virginia. During the course of it Duer denounced Meade as a "disunionist." "It is false!" shouted Meade to which Duer retorted, "You are a liar, sir!" More heated words followed as Meade rushed threateningly towards Duer, who had remained standing. The two were immediately surrounded by their friends seeking to keep them apart. An indescribable confusion resulted, with a mingling of wild threats and violent gesticulations, calls for order, and loud demands for adjournment.

Thomas J. Campbell, Clerk of the previous House, who was presiding, repeatedly called for order but general pandemonium continued to reign until Nathan Sargent, the appropriately named incumbent Sergeant at Arms,

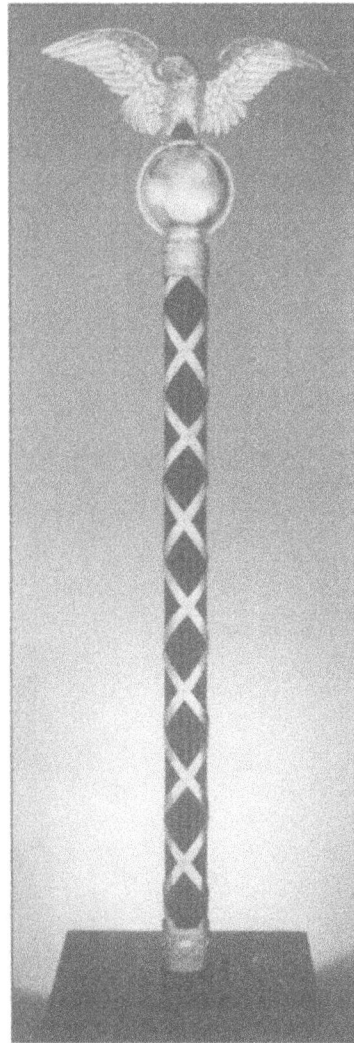

FIGURE 15
Full length view of the mace
of the House of Representatives,
made by William Adams in 1842.

---

[31] U.S. Congress, *Congressional Globe*, 27th Congress, 2nd session, p. 71.

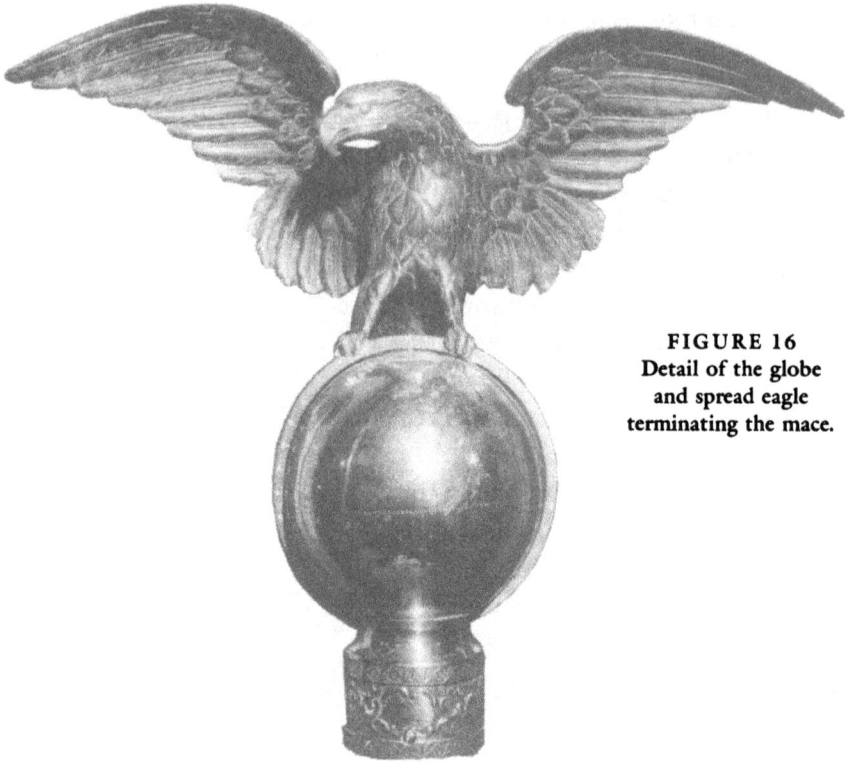

FIGURE 16
Detail of the globe
and spread eagle
terminating the mace.

FIGURE 17
Maker's inscription
on the base of
the House mace.

FIGURE 18
The House mace displayed on its pedestal at the right side of the Speaker's chair.

seized the mace from its stand and holding it high, descended among the crowd. He was greeted by cries of "Take away the mace – it has no authority here!" Duer managed to obtain a hearing at last, stating he would continue his remarks. After the House had been brought to order once more, Winthrop was elected Speaker, Sargent replaced the mace on its pedestal, and the newly selected Speaker proceeded to swear in new members.[32]

Eruptions of violent temper among many of the frontier members on the House floor were frequent, to such an extent that the House came to be referred to as "the Bear Garden" as a consequence of its frenzied partisanship, brawls and duels. One of the most memorable encounters occurred on February 5th, 1858 in the course of the angry procedural debate on the bill for Kansas statehood under the Lecompton Constitution. The House had been kept in session all night, and the Representatives were tired and worn out. Those who could secure sofas enjoyed naps between roll-calls while others visited committee rooms containing private supplies of refreshments. A struggle ensued over whether the President's Message or the Lecompton Constitution of Kansas should be referred to the Committee on Territories, controlled by a Democratic majority, or to a select committee of fifteen. John A. Quitman (D) from Mississippi had the floor, and as the discussion went on after midnight, the press reported,

> The 'Western delegates' usually hung over the backs of their chairs, displaying open mouths and giving utterance to dreadful sounds; they had learned this attitude and expression in the wayside groggeries. The 'Eastern men,' in their slumbers assumed reverential attitudes, and seemed to be lost in some devotional exercise. The 'chivalry' seemed to be restive and fighting mosquitoes, and they were, therefore, the widest awake of any of their fellow-sufferers. Speaker Orr maintained his dignified good nature, and though lost to 'outward things,' his right arm mechanically brought down his gavel upon his desk, unintentionally but truthfully indicating that the body before him was continually 'out of order.' The clerks, whose business it was to call the 'yeas' and 'nays'

---

[32] *Congressional Globe*, 31st Congress, 1st session, p. 27; Ben: Perley Poore, *Reminiscences of Sixty Years in the National Metropolis.* 2 vols. (Philadelphia: Hubbard Brothers, 1886), vol. I, pp. 532–36. Benjamin Perley Poore (1820–1887) was a popular nineteenth century newspaper correspondent, editor and author. In the sub-title of his *Reminiscences* he identified himself as "The Veteran Journalist, Clerk of the Senate Printing Records, Editor of the Congressional Directory, and Author of various Works." DAB vol. VIII, pp. 73–74.

first gabbled at their work like as many geese, then became less articulate, and finally, at their 'Herculean task,' broke down altogether. The newspaper reporters in the side galleries, under the delusion that they were in a vast oyster saloon in a state of drunken demoralization, went to cracking smutty jokes and pelting each other with spit balls, the solid contents of which were the President's Kansas message, degluted with Virginia weed and lager bier . . .

The time and the hour came. Mr. [Galusha Aaron] Grow (R), of Pennsylvania, passed over, physically to "the Democratic side of the House," for the purpose of conferring, probably about "pairing off to liquor," with Mr. [John Joseph] Hickman (D), "a Douglas Democrat," when, having finished his conference, he was passing down the side aisle, on his way back to his seat. At the moment Gen. Quitman, asked unanimous consent ". . . to submit a motion out of order" (as if a motion at that time and under those circumstances could have been anything else than *out of order*). Mr. Grow, raising himself from his somnolent state, according to the usual custom, said, "I object, Mr. Speaker; let us go on in the regular order." Whereupon, Mr. [Laurence M.] Keitt (D), of South Carolina, who was near Mr. Grow, rather roughly suggested that the gentleman should go over to his own side, if he wanted to object; whereat Mr. Grow, inflamed with the general principle of constitutional liberty, for which our ancestors principally fought and died (always excepting those who told things to both sides, and thus founded some of the oldest and wealthiest families in the country), resented this intrusion from the gentleman of the Palmetto State, and boldly and fearlessly asserted that he was in a ". . . free hall – that a man could be where he pleased in it," forgetting that he could not be in two places at the same time, nor occupy the same space already filled by an honorable gentleman – nor could he be nowhere in the hall, for nature abhors a vacuum: and with such a general but incorrect expression of the great principle of American liberty, he continued to walk slowly down the hall.

Mr. Keitt, who was probably in a somnambullic state, . . . rushed into the "area of freedom," and turning round faced up the aisle just as Mr. Grow reached the bottom of it, and with an authoritative air asked Mr. Grow what he meant by his answer: Mr. Grow under the circumstances with remarkable presence of mind, remembered what he had last said, and repeated the broad declaration that he was in a free hall. This proposition, so pertinaciously insisted upon by the gentleman from Pennsylvania, aroused Mr. Keitt's ire – for he, Mr. Keitt, knew full well that it wasn't a "free hall," that nobody had a right on the floor except members of Congress . . . and so outraged had he become, that he clenched at something in his indignation. Words now grew "fast and furious;" Grow persisted in the ridiculous idea that he could go where he pleased in the hall, implying that he could get into an inkstand or the Speaker's tobacco box; Mr. Keitt, equally enthusiastic, contradicted this often asserted proposition, and in the excitement, "fell on the floor."[33]

A member of Congress who had witnessed the altercation described "An Affray in the House," in greater detail in an interview in the popular press:

> Mr. Keitt (taking Mr. Grow by the throat), said, 'I will let you know that you are a d---d Black Republican puppy.' Mr. Grow knocked up his hand, saying, 'I shall occupy such place in this hall as I please, and no nigger driver shall crack his whip over me.' Mr. Keitt then again grabbed Mr. Grow by the throat, and Mr. Grow knocked his hand off, and Mr. Keitt coming to him again, Mr. Grow knocked him down. The fight took place at twenty minutes to two o'clock.[34]

What the press described and illustrated as "The Congressional Row" continued:

> Now the melée became general; the members who had previously been stewing and sweating in their sleep, and all probably dreaming that they were in some personal danger, like a fellow suddenly precipitated in the water, commenced "striking out." In the twinkling of an eye—very slow twinkling, it must be remembered—some forty or fifty Republicans came dashing across the hall, headed by [John Fox] Potter (R) of Wisconsin, who leaped into the midst of the arena with an agility commendable to behold, and then commenced a series of muscular demonstrations that would have been very alarming had they followed the bite of a mad dog; the effect of all this was a general distribution of side licks, back handers, and stomach winders, that acted wonderfully as specifics in waking up the gentlemen most interested. That the whole thing might have the air of an Indian pow-wow, Potter seized Barksdale (D), of Mississippi, by the hair of the head, and awful to relate, *tore the scalp entirely off*—whereupon, [Cadwallader Colden] Washburn (R), of Wisconsin, having his reminiscences of fights with the red men revived within him, pitched into the ring, causing an immense rolling over on the floor of numerous specimens of the collected wisdom of the nation.
>
> Meanwhile the speaker battered the front of his new desk into mince meat, and wore off the sharp edges of his hammer, crying out at the top of his voice, "Order! order!" which was as practical as if a katydid should

---

[33] "Congressional Row in the U.S. House of Representatives on Friday, February 5th," *Frank Leslie's Illustrated Newspaper*, vol. 5, No. 116, February 20, 1858, p. 117, 177–78.
[34] "An Affray in the House," *Harper's Weekly*, February 13, 1858, p. 102.

FIGURE 19
"The last hours of Congress, March 1859." From *Harper's Weekly*, March 12, 1859.

by its piping try to drown the thunder. The Sergeant-at-Arms, believing in the bird of Jove, seized an emblem of the valorous "critter," and rushed into the body of the hall, but as the Sergeant-at-Arms didn't bargain to prevent the members of Congress fighting and rowdying as much as they pleased, he merely waved his spread eagle over their heads, and so judiciously managed, that he left the impression that he was on both sides of the quarrel, and would no more hurt the feelings of a representative by enforcing the rules formed for the good of the House, than he would refuse the forty-ninth stiff cocktail, necessary to carry him through the fatigues of the day.

In infinitely less time than our facts can be detailed – in the short conventional space of three minutes – this flurry began and ended. As the excitement wore off the members presented the appearance of hot mutton fat suddenly brought in contact with the north wind. Every man looked more or less as if he had been caught in a dirty scrape, and only found relief in the fact that his compatriots were as guilty as himself, and therefore wouldn't peach.[35]

---

[35] "Congressional Row . . . ." *Frank Leslie's Illustrated Newspaper*, vol. 5, No. 116, February 20, 1858, pp. 117, 177–78.

FIGURE 20

"Congressional Row, in the U.S. House of Representatives, Midnight of Friday, February 5th, 1858."
From *Frank Leslie's Illustrated Newspaper*, vol. 5 No. 116, February 20, 1858, p. 117.

Poore, who also reported the event, commented, "Horrible to relate, Mr. Barksdale's wig came off in [John] Cadwalader's left hand, and his right fist expended itself with tremendous force against the unresisting air. This ludicrous incident unquestionably did much toward restoring good nature subsequently, and its effect was heightened not as little by the fact that in the excitement of the occasion Barksdale restored his wig wrong-side foremost."[36]

In this period an interesting comparison was made between the British House of Commons and the American House of Representatives by a British observer who reported and illustrated in *The Illustrated London News* in 1861. Speaking of the scene as depicted by the *News* artist, the writer commented that it ". . . is highly characteristic, and is not, as may be supposed, wholly, if at all, in caricature." He went on to note

> The contrast which it presents to our House of Commons is very striking. With us, though the appearance of members is easy enough, especially owing to their privilege of wearing their hats when seated, yet the arrangements of the seats render their attitudes, as a rule, somewhat rigid, and any comfort in the way of lounging, as well as reading or writing, is not attainable in the House proper, though there is every facility in that way in the anterooms and libraries. None of the messengers of the House are permitted to come within the bar, and the reading of a newspaper or any book, but such as are used for quotation in debate, puts a member out of order."

The observer then went on to relate that in the House of Representatives exactly the opposite prevailed. The entire floor of the chamber was occupied by desks for writing and lounging chairs; newspapers were in abundance and young boys kept running about delivering letters and messages. "Sometimes our legislators are noisy and excited," he commented, ". . . but no one ever saw any of them exhibiting in such poses as are depicted in our illustration, which, looking at the comparative unconcern which appears to prevail, seem to be nothing extraordinary in the Transatlantic Assembly."[37]

An event that occurred in 1877 in the House during the second session of the 44th Congress would seem to bear out the description by the British visitor, and was featured in the press in an article entitled

---

[36] Poore, vol. I, pp. 532–35.

[37] "*The Hall of Representatives*, Washington," *The Illustrated London News*, April 6, 1861, p. 320.

FIGURE 21
"Incidents of the Fight by Night." From B. Perley Poore, *Reminiscences*, vol. II.

FIGURE 22

"Scene in the House of Representatives, Washington." From *The Illustrated London News*, April 6, 1861.

"The Warning of the Mace." It occurred on the evening of January 31st, during a special session of the House held for the purpose of introducing a memorial of the Florida legislature so that it could be referred by vote to the Commission. A scene developed that was so unusual that the public was expected to look upon a pictorial representation of it as a particular novelty. While the Democrats attempted to have the memorial received and referred to the Commission, the Republicans not only protested against the proposed action, but indulged in parliamentary tactics to defeat the passage, resulting in great confusion. Speaker Randall repeatedly rapped his gavel to secure the attention of the Representatives and restore orderly conduct, but his admonitions went unheeded, as members continued their loud conversation while running from desk to desk. Mr. [Horace Francis] Page of California, moved to adjourn the House to Friday, but the Speaker pointed out at once that a law compelled a meeting of the two Houses on the morrow, for a specified purpose – to count the Electoral vote – and that therefore Mr. Page's motion was out of order. The Speaker again rapped for order, without response.

> He then took the preliminary step to enforce his commands, directing one of the stalwart sergeants-at-arms to proceed with the mace of the House to the scene of the greatest uproar . . . It is a custom that has been seldom carried out, for the Speaker to give the order for such action when a member or members refuse to acknowledge his authority and submit to his demands for quietness. The officer called upon to carry the mace takes that emblem of warning in both hands, holding it before him. Standing for a moment before the Speaker's desk, and facing the House, he walks slowly to the seat of the contumacious member, pauses a while, and then, slowly retracing his steps to the bar, bows to the Speaker, as if reporting the execution of the command, replaces the mace, and takes his usual station. Should the offending member, after having been thus warned, continue his insubordination, the sergeant-at-arms, at a second command, marches solemnly to the seat of the honorable Representative, and arrests him . . .
>
> Even in the excitement of legislative debates it is rarely that the warning is found necessary, and it is far more seldom that the ceremony fails to create the anticipated effect, and render the extreme punishment of arrest obligatory upon the sergeant-at-arms.
>
> On the occasion illustrated, the confusion was so widespread that the mace-bearer did not succeed in restoring quiet, for to do so he would have been kept prancing about the vast Hall for an hour, thrusting his weapon in the faces of two-thirds of the members. The reading of Mr.

Thompson's Florida report was begun, but neither the Clerk's voice nor Mr. Thompson's could be heard amid the din and cries of "louder," "order," and motions to adjourn from the Republican side.

The reading of the bill completed, the Speaker entertained a motion to adjourn until the following noon, rather than place the majority of the members under arrest.[38]

Similar encounters occurred from time to time. During the 46th Congress in 1880, a battle was about to erupt between Representatives William A. J. Sparks (D) of Illinois and J. B. Weaver (D) of Iowa, as they approached each other with threatening gestures, and shouting menacing words. "I denounce the gentleman personally as a liar on the floor of this House!" "You are a scoundrel," Sparks responded, "and a villain and a liar." Upon which Weaver approached Sparks in a menacing manner and told him, "If you get within my reach I will hit you!" Other members felt compelled to intervene, and as many rose to their feet and moved forward to separate them, some of them interposed themselves between them. The Speaker thereupon took the chair, in the belief that he was justified in doing so by parliamentary propriety and practice, announcing that he had done so for the purpose of restoring order. Then the Sergeant at Arms, by order of the Speaker, quickly moved about the House to the scene of contention bearing the mace, and order reigned once more.[39]

Another confrontation occurred on February 17, 1885, during the 48th Congress. Representative John D. White of Kentucky (R), who frequently used abusive language and whom Speaker Carlisle (D) found particularly annoying, rose to state a question of personal privilege and to disassociate himself from earlier remarks made by another member. When he was called to order by the Speaker *pro tempore* and ordered to resume his seat, White refused to do so. The Speaker thereupon stated that the Sergeant at Arms would see that the order of the Chair was obeyed. Without the mace, Mr. Hill, the Assistant Sergeant at Arms, proceeded up the aisle, and when he laid hands on White, the latter resisted.

Hill returned to the Speaker's desk, and carrying the mace, proceeded once more towards White while the Speaker announced that he would recognize no gentleman until all members had resumed their

---

[38] "The Ceremony of the Mace," *Frank Leslie's Illustrated Newspaper*, February 24, 1877, p. 497.

[39] *Congressional Record*, 46th Congress, 3rd session, p. 311; Harding, p. 6.

FIGURE 23
"The Ceremony of the Mace." The Sergeant at Arms presenting the
mace before a member of the House on the night of January 31st, 1877.
From *Frank Leslie's Illustrated Newspaper*, vol. XLIII, No. 1117, February 24, 1877.

seats. Despite repeated denials of his appeal by the Chair, White and his colleague William D. Kelley (R) of Pennsylvania continued to argue passionately that White was justified in his initial refusal to obey the Assistant Sergeant at Arms without the mace, because without that symbol the Assistant Sergeant at Arms had no authority on the floor of the House. When he was confronted with the mace, however, White again resumed his seat.[40]

Numerous instances of disorder occurred on the floor of the House in 1889 during the 51st Congress, known as "the Reed Congress," during which, by direction of the Speaker, the Sergeant at Arms paced up and down the aisles, mace in hand, to avert impending confrontations. He was again called into action in 1893, during the 53rd Congress. Representative John A. Heard (D) of Missouri became involved in a heated argument with Representative W. C. P. Breckinridge (D) of Kentucky, culminating in a brief scuffle. The Sergeant at Arms with mace in hand approached both men and brought them before the bar of the House, where eventually the participants apologized first to the House and then to each other.[41]

On occasion the weapons were more than mere spoken words. In 1899, during the 55th Congress, Charles L. Bartlett (D) of Georgia threw a volume of the *United States Statutes* at James M. Brumm of Pennsylvania, upon which Benjamin F. Russell, the mace-bearing Sergeant at Arms, successfully intervened. This was not the only occasion that the fiery Bartlett had to be so quelled. In the closing hours of a session of the 60th Congress, Representative George Southwick (R) of New York with caustic remarks expressed his grievance at the Committee on Accounts's failure to provide an increase of compensation to a House employee. Bartlett, the ranking member of the Committee, construed the remarks to be directed to himself, and brandishing a knife he rushed at Southwick. Several members intercepted him in the main aisle until Henry Casson, the Sergeant at Arms, appeared on the scene with the mace.[42]

Among the most recent encounters requiring the calming ministrations of the mace were several incidents that occurred in 1911, in the third session of the 61st Congress. During discussion on February 23rd of a bill relating to the coal lands in Alaska, Franklin W. Mondell (R)

---

[40] *Congressional Record*, 48th Congress, 2nd session, pp. 1419–20; Harding, p. 6.
[41] Harding, p. 6.
[42] Harding, pp. 6–7.

of Wisconsin moved to suspend the rules and pass the bill. Alaska Delegate James Wickersham (R) then read a letter from the Secretary of the Interior certifying that payments had been received on one hundred eighteen coal locations. Mondell, from his seat, called out that Wickersham ". . . is a liar, that is all!" Wickersham responded that Mondell was "a liar, if you say that; that is all." This exchange was followed by menacing gestures between the two, whereupon the Speaker *pro tempore* called upon the Sergeant at Arms, who advanced with the mace before him. James A. Tawney (R) of Minnesota then made a motion that the words used by Mondell and Wickersham were in violation of the rules of the House and that they should be taken down and reported from the desk and furthermore, that both should be made to apologize. Accordingly, both members presented apologies and no further action was taken.

On March 4th, in the waning hours of the same Congress, there was again considerable disorder on the floor. Speaker Joseph C. Cannon (R), after considering the conference report on the general deficiency appropriation bill, put the question on agreeing to the report. To quell the confusion that resulted, he ordered the Sergeant at Arms to take the mace and see that all members were seated, while the Clerk read the roll call. Members took their seats and the vote continued without further interruption.[43]

A Representative who required the mace on more than one occasion was Thomas Heflin (D) of Alabama. In 1916, during the 65th Congress, he exchanged ugly words with Representative Patrick Daniel Norton (R) of North Dakota, who thereupon belligerently approached him, but the Sergeant at Arms, Robert B. Gordon, came between them with the mace before further damage was done. During the same hectic session Heflin, who strongly advocated war with Germany, offered some remarks that were construed to be casting aspersions on the patriotism of John L. Burnett from his own state, one of the members opposed to the passage of the resolution that brought the United States into World War I. Burnett thereupon inquired why Heflin did not go to war himself. The heated exchange that ensued was effectively terminated by presentation of the mace.[44]

From time to time the mace was also called into service to bring in absentees from night sessions of the House. Although in general

---

[43] *Congressional Record*, 61st Congress, 3rd session, 1911, pp. 3235, 4330–31.
[44] Harding, p. 7.

FIGURE 24

"The Sergeant at Arms bringing in Absentee Members." From *Frank Leslie's Illustrated Newspaper.*

members faithfully performed their duties during daytime sessions, they were inclined to respond to social claims in the evenings with the consequence that at times the House was without a quorum. It then became necessary to send the Sergeant at Arms bearing the mace in search of the absentees. Such situations were described in the popular press in 1881:

> Night sessions of the House of Representatives are not infrequently attended by incidents similar to that depicted on page 9. However faithful members may be in the performance of their duties during the day sessions, they are very apt to recognize the claims of "society" in the evening, preferring the attractions of the dinner-table, ball or reception, to the hard routine of debate and roll-call. The House is thus sometimes left without a quorum, and it becomes necessary to send the Sergeant at Arms after absentees. These are seized wherever they could be found, and marched away to the House – possibly from the 'wine and walnuts' of a secretary's or ambassador's table and in full evening dress, only to be greeted by the jeers of their more industrious but less fortunate associates to whom the banquet board offers its kindly solicitations.
>
> In one case, a year or so ago, a dinner-party composed of leading Democrats and Republicans – Senators and Representatives – who had reached only the third or fourth course at the table of an epicurean host, was suddenly pounced upon by a House official, greatly to their consternation. The butler managed for a time to moderate the demands of the intruder by a vigilant display of hospitality, but in the end, even his attentions lost their spell, and the diners, for whom the House waited, were led off in triumph – by that time mellow and merry enough to enjoy themselves the joke of which they were the victims.[45]

House rules require that the mace be present on every occasion on which the House of Representatives meets officially, even when such meetings take place outside the House chamber. Following presidential elections every four years, for example, the inaugurations take place with the Congress officially in attendance in the meeting place of the Congress. The members of the House and of the Senate process as separate entities to the ceremony and take seats of honor behind the podium. The body of the House of Representatives is led by the Sergeant at Arms or his assistant carrying the mace. Once the Representatives are in place, he then stands behind the members throughout

---

[45] "How Absentees are Brought to the House," *Frank Leslie's Illustrated Newspaper*, vol. LII, No. 1327, March 5, 1881, pp. 9 and 11.

FIGURE 25
The procession of the House mace during the Presidential Inauguration, 1969.

FIGURE 26
Transportation of the House
mace from the Capitol to the
Smithsonian Institution
on January 20, 1977.

the ceremony as a visible symbol of the authority of the House upon this most official of occasions.[46]

The venerable mace had served its function faithfully for one hundred thirty years, when in 1974 it was discovered that some of its components had become dangerously loose and shaken as a consequence of handling during its long years of use. Its disability derived principally from the fact that the device had not been originally designed to be placed erect upon a base. Although shortly after the new mace had been installed an additional support had been added to the base for the purpose, the central wooden shaft no longer provided sufficient stability. Accordingly arrangements were made to have the necessary repairs undertaken by skilled technicians on the staff of the National Museum of History and Technology (now the National Museum of American History) of the Smithsonian Institution. The treasured relic was taken to the Museum with appropriate precautions during one of the periods that the House was not in session. The weakened central wooden shaft was replaced with a bronze rod that provided the required strength, and other minor repairs, none of which affected the mace's visual appearance, were satisfactorily completed before the relic was returned to the House.[47]

---

[46] *The Mace*, p. 13.

[47] Communication from George M. White, Architect of the Capitol, to Robert M. Organ, Chief, Conservation-Analytical Laboratory, December 3, 1974; *The Washington Evening Star*, United Press International Release, October 19, 1974, "Hill Mace is Being Repaired;" Smithsonian Conservation-Analytical Laboratory, *Report CAL 1917*, November 4, 1974; Associated Press Release, November 11, 1974, "House Mace Returns After Repair Trip."

FIGURE 27
The House mace dismantled in preparation for repair
at the Smithsonian Institution Conservation Analytical Laboratory.

THE GAVEL
OF THE
UNITED STATES SENATE

In order to judge of the form to be given to [the Senate], it will
be proper to take a view of the ends to be served by it. These were
first to protect the people against their rulers; secondly to protect
the people against the transient impressions into which they
themselves might be led.

JAMES MADISON [JUNE 26, 1787][48]

AT THE SAME TIME that the House of Representatives was appointing a Sergeant at Arms and selecting a mace, similar considerations were taking place in the Senate. On April 7, 1789, the day following establishment of their first quorum and the organization of the Senate into a legislative body, the position of "Doorkeeper" was created, the first elected official of that body. It was a significant position, for the public was barred from the Senate's proceedings which were kept secret until December 1795. The first to be appointed to the position was the Irish-born James Mathers, who had served in the Continental Army under General Washington and was wounded several times. For his valor he had been appointed sergeant at arms and doorkeeper of the Continental Congress before his appointment to the Senate. He served in the position for almost twenty-three years, having all the responsibilities of a sergeant at arms at first but without that title nor a symbol of his office.[49]

It is possible that the Senators conceived of having a second position to carry a mace, for several weeks later the body reviewed the application of William Finnie for the position of ". . . Mace bearer to ye Senate." During the American Revolution Finnie had served as Deputy

---

[48] James Madison, June 26, 1787. *Notes of Debates in the Federal Convention of 1787 Reported by James Madison*, p. 193.

[49] Linda Grant De Pauw, C. B. Bickford and LaVonne M. Siegel, eds., *Documentary History of the First Federal Congress of the United States of America, March 4, 1789–March 3, 1791.* 2 vols. (Baltimore: The Johns Hopkins University Press, 1972), vol. I, pp. 23, 42; George H. Haynes, *The Senate of the United States. Its History and Practice.* 2 vols. (Boston: Houghton Mifflin Company, 1938), vol. 2, p. 263; *National Intelligencer* (Washington, D.C.), September 5, 1811.

Quartermaster General of the Southern Department. The journal of the Senate recorded that on April 22nd ". . . the petition of William Finnie, praying that he might be appointed Serjeant at Arms, was read." The application was not taken up at that time, but a plan to establish the formal position of a sergeant at arms was unquestionably in the minds of at least one faction of that august body.[50]

The proposal to appoint such an official was made by Senator Richard Henry Lee, and supported by Vice President John Adams. As reported by William Maclay, on May 12th Adams delivered a speech ". . . on the subject of our having a Sergeant at Arms. He seemed to wish that the officer should be Usher of the Black Rod. He described this officer as appurtenant to the House of Lords. . . ." The suggestion made by Adams drew a negative response from Maclay as well as others.[51]

Fresh from several years abroad, chiefly in England, as American minister, it was felt by some that the European sojourn had somewhat modified Adams's native republican outlook. He was concerned and confused about the selection of nomenclature for the solons of the new government, and at one point he expressed his distress by the fact that ". . . I am Vice President. In this I am nothing, but I may be everything. But I am president also of the Senate. When the President comes into the Senate, what shall I be? I cannot be [president] then." He visualized the Senate to be comparable to the British House of Lords, and suggested that senators be given the title of "Right Honorable" in the minutes, and proposed the institution of a form of the mace for the Senate that was similar to the one adopted for the House of Lords.

"The Gentleman Usher of the Black Rod" is the Chief Gentleman Usher of the Lord Chamberlain's department of the British royal household, serving as a personal attendant of the sovereign in the upper House and also as usher of the Order of the Garter, the doorkeeper at meetings of the knights' Chapter. He derives his title from his traditional staff of office, which consists of an ebony wand, or form of mace, surmounted by a golden lion. The position was initiated in

[50] *Journal of the First Session of the Senate of the United States of America. Begun and Held at the City of New York, March 4, 1789* . . . (Washington, D.C.: Gales & Seaton, 1820), April 22, 1789, p. 15, 23; The Library of Congress, Manuscripts Division, *The Papers of George Washington*, c. 1789, fol. 1783, applications addressed to William Grayson.

[51] C. A. Beard, ed. *The Journal of William Maclay, United States Senator from Pennsylvania, 1789–1791* (New York: Albert & Charles Boni, 1927), pp. 3, 31.

1350, and appointment is made by royal letters patent. His duties correspond to those of the serjeant-at-arms in the House of Commons. He is responsible for maintaining order in the House of Lords, with power to arrest any peer guilty of breach of privilege or other offense of which the House takes cognizance.

The Gentleman Usher's most prominent function is the summoning of the House of Commons and their speaker to the upper House to hear an address from the throne, or royal assent given to bills. On such occasions the Usher becomes the central figure in an unusual ceremony. As soon as the attendants of the House of Commons become aware of his approach, the doors are closed in his face. The Gentleman Usher then strikes the doors three times with his staff of office, and on being asked, "Who is there?" he replies "Black Rod" and is admitted. Advancing to the bar, he makes three obeisances, then addresses the speaker, informing him that the king commands the House to attend him immediately in the House of Lords. The exchange that takes place with the closing of the doors to the Gentleman Usher is a formality that originated in 1642 with the famous attempt of King Charles I to arrest five members of the House of Commons, and signifies the right of the House of Commons to maintain its freedom of speech and uninterrupted debate.[52]

Despite the urgings of the Lee-Adams faction, a position of a Sergeant at Arms or mace-bearer was not then instituted in the Senate, and that position's functions continued to be performed by the Doorkeeper. It was not until almost a decade later, on February 5, 1798, however, that the title of the incumbent was officially changed to "Doorkeeper and Sergeant at Arms" of the Senate. Eventually the first part of the title was dropped. The incumbent's duties were virtually identical to those of the Sergeant at Arms of the House of Representatives, and were clearly defined, to ". . . execute the Senate's orders as to decorum both on the floor of the Chamber and in the galleries. He takes persons into custody in case of contempt of the Senate; arrests and detains them as ordered; and hales absentees into the Senate Chamber when required to do so, to complete a quorum. He is responsible for the enforcement of all rules made for the regulation of the Senate Wing of the Capitol." As the 1st Congress was about to adjourn on March 3, 1791, it passed a resolution further defining Mathers's

---

[52] *Encyclopedia Britannica*, 1943, vol. IV, pp. 24–25.

responsibilities to include proper maintenance of the Senate chamber and committee rooms in their absence ". . . and also to make the necessary provision of fire wood for the next Session."[53]

The mace was not adopted by the Senate. Whereas in the House of Representatives the body's legislative authority lies in the symbolism of the mace, in the Senate it resides only in the person of its Sergeant at Arms. As with the Sergeant at Arms of the House, since 1798 the primary responsibility of the Senate's Sergeant at Arms has been to secure the presence of Senators in the Senate chamber when the body's business had been halted due to lack of a quorum, apart from the Senate's statutory provisions and rule for encouraging attendance. In the earlier years his orders were couched in somewhat peremptory language, the incumbent being directed forthwith to ". . . summon and command the absent members to be and appear before the Senate immediately" and furthermore to ". . . take all practicable means to enforce their attendance."[54]

On February 5, 1798, in preparation for the impeachment trial of Senator William Blount for conspiring with the British to incite Indians to seize frontier lands, it further clarified the Doorkeeper's responsibilities. It specified that he was ". . . hereby invested with the authority of Sergeant-at-Arms, to hold said office during the pleasure of the Senate, whose duty it shall be to execute the commands of the Senate, from time to time, and all such process as shall be directed to him by the President of the Senate." A warrant was then issued for Blount's arrest and Mathers traveled to Tennessee to find him. When state authorities assured him that Blount could not be taken from the state, however, Mathers returned the warrant to the Senate, and the impeachment trial proceeded. Several months later the Senate added provisions in no uncertain terms empowering the sergeant at arms to bring in absent members in the absence of a quorum.

Later, by the middle of the nineteenth century, the Senate's order was expressed in more cautious and guarded terms, ". . . the Sergeant-at-Arms be directed to *request* the attendance of absent members." A motion, in the absence of a quorum, that the Sergeant at Arms

---

[53] De Pauw et al., vol. I, p. 700; Haynes, p. 263; Robert C. Byrd, *The Senate 1789–1989. Addresses on the History of the United States Senate, Senate Document 100-20.* 4 vols. (Washington: U.S. Printing Office, 1988), vol. II, pp. 281–84. The change was made on March 3, 1805.

[54] Jonathan Elliot, *The Debates in the Several State Conventions on the Adoption of the Federal Constitution.* 4 vols. (New York, 1836), vol. 4, p. 130; Byrd, vol. II, pp. 281–84.

FIGURE 28
Portrait of Senator William Blount of Tennessee,
the first member to be expelled from the Senate.

". . . compel the attendance of absentees" was ruled out as late as 1872 on the basis that inasmuch as the Senate had made no provision in its rules for compelling attendance of absent members, it was not in the power of a minority of the Senate to change the existing rule on the subject.[55]

The problem was resolved by adopting a rule that provided that if the question is raised at any time during the daily session requiring the presence of a quorum, without debate the roll is to be called and the result announced. If the roll call reveals the absence of a quorum, ". . . a majority of the Senators present may direct the Sergeant at Arms

---

[55] *Congressional Globe*, 42nd Congress, 2nd session, pp. 2627–29, Byrd, vol. II, pp. 282–83.

to request and, when necessary, to compel the attendance of the absent Senators, which order shall be determined without debate. . . ." In 1877 the Senators voted that the Sergeant at Arms must first be required to request before being directed to compel attendance of absent Senators, but when the point was raised in 1915, the presiding officer ruled that it was quite in order to compel attendance of absent Senators before requesting them to return.[56]

The Senate chamber occasionally also became the scene of conflict between Senators, sometimes taking the form of invective and at other times of stronger measures. On all such occasions, the Senate's Sergeant at Arms nonetheless fulfills his function merely by his presence at the scene on the Senate floor.

Among the least charismatic Congressional personalities was the wealthy slave owner Senator John Randolph of Roanoke from Virginia, who was described as ". . . one of the most brilliant, arrogant, deranged and pathetic men of his time." This lean, haughty Virginian generally sporting the most eccentric costume was accustomed to stride into the old Senate chamber trailed by his noisy hounds, snapping a riding whip in one hand and bearing a cup of porter in the other, mesmerizing and terrorizing all whom he encountered. After having served several terms in the House, he moved to the Senate in 1825 to fill a vacancy. Although an electrifying speaker, his demonic diatribes of hate-filled language flavored with occasional glimpses of brilliance, often lasted for several hours. His performance brought many visitors to the galleries to hear him, although it did not win him friends among the senators, particularly those from the north. His hatred of President John Quincy Adams was exceeded only by that for the President's father and for Henry Clay.

In March 1826 Randolph had his opportunity for revenge against all three, on the subject of participation in the Panama Congress of South America, which President Adams had accepted without consultation with the Senate. Randolph compared the union of Adams and Clay to disreputable characters in Henry Fielding's novel *Tom Jones*, shocking and stunning the senators, and as a consequence of which Clay challenged Randolph to a duel. Neither being expert in the use of arms when they met on April 8, 1826, both men missed in the first exchange of shots. In the second round Clay's bullet cut through Randolph's overcoat. Randolph then fired into the air, tossed his pistol

[56] *Congressional Record*, 44th Congress, 2nd session, pp. 690–93; Haynes, pp. 264, 350–53; Byrd, vol. II, pp. 284–85.

FIGURE 29
Senator John Randolph of Roanoke in Virginia, striding into
the Senate chamber with his dogs.

aside, and held out his hand to Clay, saying, "You owe me a coat, Mr. Clay," to which the latter replied, "I am glad that the debt is no greater."[57]

---

[57] Poore, vol. I, p. 69; George Dangerfield, *The Era of Good Feelings* (New York: Harcourt Brace, 1952), pp. 354–58, 363–64; Margaret L. Coit, *John C. Calhoun, American Portrait* (Boston: Houghton Mifflin Company, 1950), p. 150; Byrd, vol. I, pp. 90–93.

Another example of violence in the Senate took place in April 1828, when a journalist named Russell Jarvis responded roughly to a rude remark made to him at the White House several days previously by John Adams, son of President John Quincy Adams then serving as his father's secretary. As young Adams was walking from the House to the Senate through the Capitol Rotunda bearing an official message from his father to the Senate, Jarvis assaulted him. Later he claimed the encounter was accidental, that he was unaware that Adams was on official business, and that he had merely pulled Adams' nose and slapped his face. President Adams was outraged and demanded redress from both the House and the Senate. As a consequence, the incident led to the establishment of the U.S. Capitol Police force.[58]

One of the Senate's most notable violent exchanges occurred in the 1850s with the opposition between Thomas Hart Benton of Missouri and Henry Foote of Mississippi on the subject of abolition. When Foote accused Benton of attacking the late John C. Calhoun, Benton strode down the aisle towards him, Foote retreated meanwhile drawing his gun. "I have no pistols!" Benton proclaimed, "I disdain to carry arms. Stand out of the way, and let the assassin fire!" The gun was quickly removed from Foote, and as everyone was made to be seated, peace was restored once more. Foote went unpunished, but as a consequence of the adverse publicity made future formal exchanges between them comparatively civil. Later Foote threatened to write a "little" book about Benton, to which the latter responded that he in turn would produce a "large" book–in which Foote would have no part whatever." Each kept his word.[59]

Even greater violence marked an incident on the Senate floor in 1856 when Senator Charles Sumner of Massachusetts, who supported Kansas as a free state, denounced the Kansas-Nebraska Act as a swindle, and cast aspersions on Senator Stephen Douglas and Senator Andrew Butler of South Carolina, during the latter's absence from the chamber. Following adjournment, Representative Preston Brooks, one of Butler's South Carolina kinsman, discovered Sumner working alone in the Senate chamber. Accusing Sumner of having libeled his state, Brooks raised his cane and furiously brought it down again and again on Sumner's head. Dazed from the blows and blinded by blood

[58] *Register of Debates*, 20th Congress, 1st session, pp. iii, 810; *Niles Weekly Register*, April 26, 1828; Byrd, vol. I, pp. 100–1.
[59] Elbert B. Smith, *Magnificent Missourian, Thomas Hart Benton* (Philadelphia: 1958), pp. 269–72; Byrd, vol. I, pp. 90–93, 195–96.

FIGURE 30

Cartoon by Edward Clay of the encounter between Senators Thomas Hart Benton and Henry Foote during the debate on the Compromise of 1850.

SOUTHERN CHIVALRY — ARGUMENT versus CLUB'S.

FIGURE 31
Senator Charles Sumner being beaten by Representative Preston Brooks in May 1856,
portrayed by a Northern cartoonist.

streaming down his face, Sumner raised himself holding on to his desk, which was bolted to the floor, ripping it loose as he attempted to stand. Brooks continued to beat him until the cane was smashed into fragments. Others rushed to help Sumner, a physician was summoned, and although the wounds were serious, they proved to be not fatal.[60]

In late 1942 those engaged in the filibuster by Mississippi's senator Theodore Bilbo (D) relating to the poll tax urged senators to go home so that an adjournment could be forced by lack of a quorum. Determined to obtain a quorum at any cost, the majority leader Senator Alben W. Barkley (D) thereupon offered a successful motion to instruct the Sergeant at Arms to arrest eight senators who had absented themselves from the chamber although remaining in the city. The task of arresting Tennessee's Senator Kenneth McKellar (D) fell to J. Mark Trice, Assistant Sergeant at Arms. Uncertain of his instructions, Trice inquired whether it was Senator McKellar that he was to arrest. "I mean *everyone!*" Barkley promptly replied, and although it was in the middle of the night, Trice set out for the Mayflower Hotel. McKellar

---

[60] *Bassett Papers*, Box 1, p. 168; *Congressional Globe*, 24th Congress, 1st session, Appendix, pp. 280–89; David Donald, *Charles Sumner and the Coming of the Civil War* (New York: Alfred A. Knopf, 1960), p. 278; Byrd, vol. I, pp. 209–11.

did not answer his knock but with the assistance of a hotel official, Trice found him in his room. The old senator agreed to accompany him back to Capitol Hill, and it did not become necessary for Trice to mention or use the subpoena he had carried in his pocket. It was not until they had almost reached their destination, however, that the senator realized he was about to help Barkley obtain a quorum that might defeat his fellow Southerners. He was so angry at Barkley that months passed before he would speak to him again.[61]

The Senate Sergeant at Arms has power to arrest not only members of the Senate, but others as well. On occasion he was sent out to locate and bring in witnesses reluctant to testify before the Senate as a whole or before one of its committees. One of the earliest such incidents occurred in 1800 with William Duane, editor of the *Aurora and General Advertiser* of Philadelphia, and again in 1848 when John Nugent, Washington correspondent for the *New York Herald* was held for leaking the still secret Treaty of Guadalupe-Hidalgo. In 1871 the Sergeant at Arms held two reporters of the *New York Times* while waiting for them to reveal their source for the still secret Treaty of Washington. More recently, in 1951 the Sergeant at Arms Joe Duke rounded up one of Al Capone's mobsters, Jacob Guzik, who had been summoned to testify before the Kefauver crime investigating committee. On occasion the Sergeant at Arms has even served as jailer, of newspaper correspondents who had published Senate secrets, for example, and who were held prisoner in committee rooms because they would not divulge their sources. As the major law enforcement official of the Senate, the Sergeant at Arms can be empowered to arrest not only any member of the Senate, but also the Senate's president and in fact even the President of the United States. It was the Senate Sergeant at Arms, George T. Brown, who in March 1868 notified President Andrew Johnson of his impeachment trial in the Senate chamber and served him with a subpoena.[62]

As does the Sergeant at Arms of the House, the Senate's counterpart

[61] Richard Langham Riedel, *Halls of the Mighty* (Washington: Robert B. Luce, Inc., 1969), pp. 89–90; Polly Ann Davis, *Alben B, Barkley Senate Majority Leader and Vice President* (New York: Garland Publishing Co., 1979), pp. 114–17; Byrd vol. I, pp. 520–21.

[62] F. B. Marbut, *News From the Capital. The Story of Washington Reporting* (Carbondale, Ill.: Southern Illinois University Press, 1971), pp. 89–90, 145; *Harper's Weekly*, March 28, 1868; *The Washington Post*, February 25, 1988 and April 29, 1951; Thomas W. Howard, "Peter G. Van Winkle's Vote in the Impeachment of Andrew Johnson: A West Virginian as a Profile of Courage," *West Virginia History*, July 1974, pp. 290–95; Byrd, vol. I, pp. 272–75, 286–90.

FIGURE 32
Senate Sergeant at Arms George T. Brown presenting a subpoena to
President Andrew Johnson notifying him of his impeachment trial in the Senate chamber.

also leads the formal procession of the Senate in ceremonial events, such as joint sessions of both houses, funerals, and inaugurations.

From the first meeting of the Continental Congress until the convening of the first Federal Congress, the responsible lawmakers were deeply concerned that their new government and its components should remain democratic in every sense of its meaning, and that these concerns were to be reflected in appropriate symbols. Failing to provide the office of the Doorkeeper, nor later to the Sergeant at Arms, with a symbol of his office the authority of the Senate inadvertently became vested from the very beginning in a simple device serving as a gavel wielded by the individual presiding. Consisting of a simple block of solid ivory turned somewhat in the shape of a time glass, the Senate "gavel" functions more in the nature of a knocker to bring the body to attention. According to legend, this relic has been used to call the Senate to order since its first sessions held in the spring of 1789.

Considerably less of the origins of the Senate "gavel" is known than of the mace of the House. Contemporary accounts relate that in meetings of the Continental Congress a bell and not a gavel was used. Whether John Adams, as the first Vice President to preside over the Senate of the Federal Congress, used this "gavel" cannot be determined. When he presided over the Senate in Congress Hall in Philadelphia it is said that he customarily brought that body to order by rapping a pencil upon his water glass. If he had followed the same procedure earlier in New York, then the first to use the ivory "gavel" was Thomas Jefferson after he succeeded Adams to that office.[63]

Much of the "gavel's" early history relies on recollections of Captain Isaac Bassett. Appointed a page in the Senate in 1831 by Daniel Webster, he continued to serve in the Senate until his retirement at the end of the nineteenth century. In his reminiscences, compiled at about the time of his retirement, Bassett wrote, "The same gavel which called the Senate to order in the days of Webster is in use today. It consists simply of a small *cube* of ivory like the head of a mallet without any handle. It has been used by all the Vice-Presidents as far back as I can remember." Elsewhere he noted, "Before the Senate convened, we would take turns unlocking the Vice President's desk to bring out the original ivory gavel which every Vice president, including John Adams and Thomas Jefferson,

---

[63] Communication to the writer from the late Harold L. Peterson, Chief Curator, National Park Service, July 2, 1974.

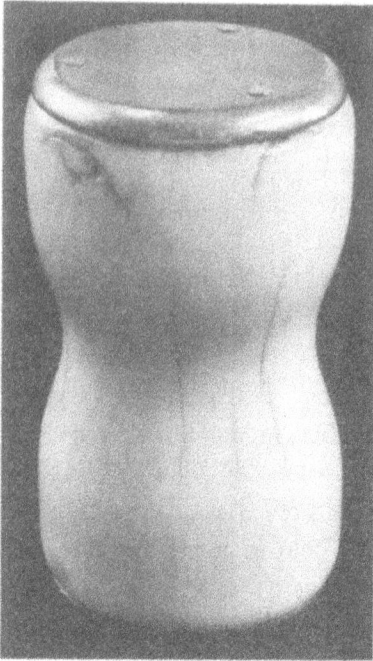

FIGURE 33
Original ivory gavel or "knocker"
of the Senate of the United States.

had used while presiding over the Senate. Shaped like an hour glass, it conveniently fit the hand."[64]

The lack of a handle for the so-called "gavel" came to public attention from time to time in the press, and in response numerous offers were made to replace it with a new one. In 1889 the The Washington Post published an interview with Senator John J. Ingalls (R) of Kansas, on the subject. Ingalls had reacted to the rash conclusions reached when it was noted that he wielded a gavel the handle of which was lacking, and to the offers to provide a replacement made by patriotic citizens. The gavel was not dilapidated, he claimed. "As a matter of fact," he commented, "that gavel never had a handle. It is in just as good condition today as it ever was. Its origin and its history are not known beyond the fact that it is a section of an elephant's tooth; that it was in use in the Senate fifty-six years ago, when Capt. Bassett first entered the service, and that even at that remote period it was looked upon as a venerable heritage from old antiquity. It may have served as a paper weight on Buddha's desk when the old patriarch lived. One thing is certain, it is a good serviceable gavel yet. Age has not made it obsolete. On the contrary, every additional day adds to its associations and increases its interest. Order, you know, was Heaven's first law, and this venerable elephant's tooth has been rapping for order so long that it seems quite possible that it may have been Heaven's first gavel and that there may never be another one like it."[65]

The ivory gavel is customarily kept in a locked drawer in the desk of the President of the Senate. Before each session, it is ceremoniously

[64] Captain Isaac Bassett, *Reminiscences.* Washington: Office of the Architect of the Capitol, archives. Unpublished manuscript, quoted in Riedel, p. 14; 90. United States Senate, Office of the Senate Curator, *Isaac Bassett Papers,* Box 2, folder B, p. 277, Box 7, folder F, pp. 5.

[65] "The Senatorial Gavel," *The Washington Post,* 1889, exact date not known, from among the *Isaac Bassett Papers,* Box 10, folder C, p. 81.

removed by the Senate's Sergeant at Arms, and placed upon the rostrum, and returned to safekeeping at each session's conclusion. Despite its age, the relic was maintained in good condition until well into the present century. Then one repair after another became necessary. As Richard L. Reidel reported in his volume *Halls of the Mighty*, the first recorded damage to it occurred in the 1920s. One of the Senators presiding over the body had been absent-mindedly doodling and it was subsequently discovered by the Sergeant at Arms that he had been carving the ends of the gavel with a pocket knife.[66]

In 1944 the knocker showed evidence of splintering, and repairs were made. It was continued in use, nonetheless, until in 1947 J. Mark Trice, Deputy Sergeant at Arms, discovered that the relic had suffered further damage, possibly derived from the inadvertent carving. In the summer of 1952, while the Senate was in recess, it was taken to the Washington firm of Galt & Bro., Inc. for repair. Silver disks were made and added as covers to each of the upper and lower faces by means of small silver screws. The cost of each disk was five dollars, and the labor required was completed for another ten dollars.[67]

Despite these remedial repairs, the days of the old relic were numbered. It was during a late night session of the 83rd Congress in 1954 that it received its ultimate blow. The Senate body was engaged in a heated discussion on the public use of atomic energy. Richard M. Nixon, the incumbent Vice President chairing the body, wielded the gavel sharply to bring order on the floor. As he did so, it disintegrated into several pieces in his hand. The silver screws had given way and the ivory face splintered and a large segment was separated from one of the ends. It was repaired by the Secretary of the Senate by the addition of an unsightly large brass screw.[68]

The time had come when a replacement was inevitable, and prevailing sentiment in the Senate decreed that its successor should be a

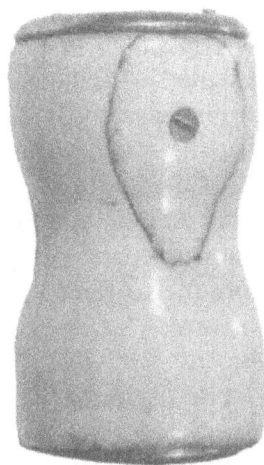

FIGURE 34
Detail of repairs
made on the Senate gavel.

---

[66] Riedel, pp. 14–15.

[67] *Report of the Secretary of the Senate for 1952*, p. 292, Item 64.

[68] William H. Honan, "Mr. President, Distinguished Colleagues . . . (The Art of Oratory in the Senate of the United States," *Esquire Magazine*, May 1969, p. 162.

suitable block of ivory to be obtained through commercial sources. This proved to be more difficult than anticipated, however, and finally the Sergeant at Arms appealed for assistance to the Embassy of India in Washington. The recently established republic of India was not only pleased to provide the ivory stock, but also arranged to have a new gavel turned from it. A model of the original was prepared and sent to India to serve as a prototype. A new gavel was duplicated in solid ivory in the same form and size as the original, except for the addition of a floral band carved in relief around its center.[69]

The Vice President of India, Sir Sarvepalli Radhakrishnam, who was later to serve as president of his country from 1962 to 1967, was sent to Washington by his government to present the new gavel in person to the United States Senate. The formal presentation was made in the Senate chamber on November 17, 1954, and the new gavel passed from the hands of the vice president of one country to those of the vice president of another. In his acceptance speech Nixon noted, ". . . for the benefit of those who have been in the galleries in the past, and those who will be there in the future, we shall place the old gavel, which no longer can be used because it is coming apart, in a box which will be kept on the Senate Rostrum, while the Senate is in session. We shall use in its place the gavel of solid ivory, which has been presented to us, it seems to me quite significantly and appropriately, by the largest democracy in the world."[70]

To maintain the two gavels side by side, a small wooden case was designed by Tillman B. Huskey, chief cabinetmaker of the Senate. Framed glazed covers individually hinged and locked were provided so that the gavels could be displayed without removing them. The case of solid Honduras mahogany was constructed in the Senate cabinet shop by Dominick Bellia, one of its craftsmen. Thereafter, each day that the Senate is in session, a page procures the case with its two gavels from the Sergeant at Arms or his Deputy, and places it upon the Senate rostrum. The new gavel is removed for use, while the relic remains on display.

The venerable old gavel was not to be permitted to retire in peace, however. Several years ago its history came to be questioned with the discovery of a document that had lain neglected among the records of the Department of the Treasury in the National Archives and Records Service. It is an invoice dated June 13, 1844 drawn to the order of

[69] *Our Capitol*, p. 29; *The Washington Daily News*, September 3, 1960, "Senate Data"; Honan, p. 162.

[70] *Congressional Record*, November 17, 1954, speech made in the Senate by Vice President Richard M. Nixon; *Our Capitol*, p. 29.

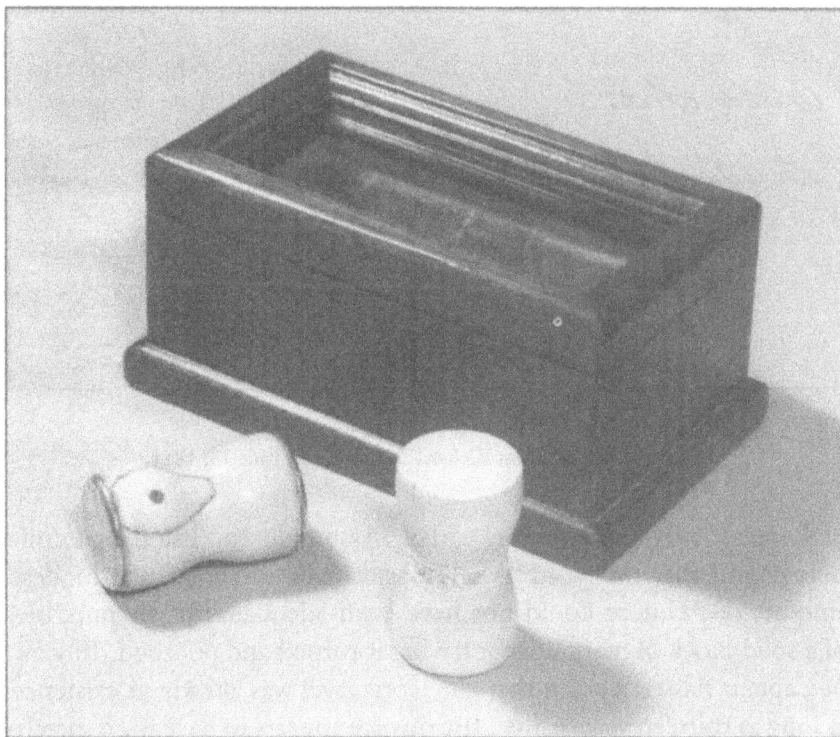

FIGURE 35
Solid ivory gavel presented to Vice President Nixon by the Vice President of India,
shown with original gavel and storage case.

the United States Senate by Richard Patten of Washington, D.C., sub-mitted for payment "To 1 Ivory Mace for Senate Chamber. . . . $4.00." The invoice was receipted by Patten as having received payment of the specified amount on July 12th from Asbury Dickim, Secretary of the Senate.[71]

Patten was a prominent maker and dealer of mathematical instru-ments who had moved to Washington from New York in about 1840 to work for the United States Coast Survey. He had repaired instru-ments for the Survey as early as 1834 and consequently his name was known in government circles. It is difficult to evaluate the significance of Patten's invoice, but it is most likely that the word "mace" was used inadvertently in place of "gavel," a confusion that may have derived from publicity attending the acquisition of a new mace by the House

[71] National Archives, *File 90, 791*, Document No. 39, invoice to the United States Senate from Richard Patten, June 13, 1844, communication to the writer from the late Julian P. Boyd, July 31, 1975.

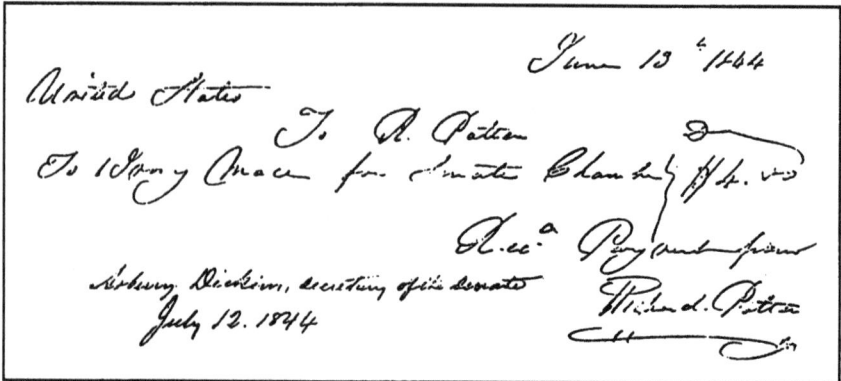

FIGURE 36
Receipted invoice from Richard Patten dated June 13, 1844.

of Representatives three years earlier. Assuming confusion in terminology and that the word "gavel" was actually intended, the modest amount of payment could not have been adequate for the purchase of a solid block of ivory nor for having it turned and polished. In view of Captain Bassett's claim that the ivory gavel was already in existence as long as thirteen years earlier, the invoice appears to have been merely for a repair made to the existing gavel not elsewhere recorded.[72]

The Senate gavel is certainly equal in age and use to its counterpart, the House's mace, and believed to be considerably older. Not only the authority of the Congress of the United States, but also the principles selected by the founding fathers in forming the new republic, are vividly reflected in the histories of these symbols of legislative authority in a democracy.

---

[72] *Washington City Directories* for 1842–1865; Silvio A. Bedini, *Thinkers and Tinkers. Early American Men of Science* (New York: Charles Scribner's Sons, 1975), pp. 361–62, 368–69; Charles E. Smart, *The Makers of Surveying Instruments in America Since 1700* (Troy, N.Y.: Regal Art Press, 1962), pp. 114–15; Roger G. Gerry, "Richard Patten: Mathematical Instrument Maker," *Antiques*, July 1959, pp. 56–58.

A FOOTNOTE TO HISTORY

THE AMERICAN PHILOSOPHICAL SOCIETY'S GAVEL

IN JUNE 1974, the late Julian P. Boyd, then editor-in-chief of *The Papers of Thomas Jefferson* and president of the American Philosophical Society, was seeking a symbol for the presidency of the Society, a position that Jefferson had honored for seventeen years. "We have no gavel of any significance," he wrote, "and there has been no symbolic transference of honors and duties from one incumbent to the next. I intend to do something about this and I thought that a gavel would be the most appropriate symbol. There is none that was used by Jefferson at Williamsburg, Richmond, or the University of Virginia. I doubt if there is one in the United States Senate and even if there were it would symbolize his presiding over that body when it was outraging him with its violations of the First Amendment."[73]

After an unsuccessful search for an appropriate symbol, Boyd subsequently concluded that a reproduction of the Senate gavel would most appropriately serve his purpose, since the Senate gavel had been used by Vice President Jefferson in the Senate when it met in the building across the square from the Society's headquarters. "It could serve as a symbol of the impartiality with which he presided over a body whose legislation outraged every principle he stood for," Boyd decided, and proceeded with arrangements to obtain permission to have the original copied.[74]

Boyd's request addressed to the Honorable William H. Wannall, Sergeant at Arms of the Senate, for permission to have a reproduction made was accompanied by a letter he had received from the Commission on Art and Antiquities of the United States Senate, signed jointly by Senators Mike Mansfield (D), Chairman, and Hugh Scott (R), Vice Chairman. "Because of the historic ties that existed between the early Congress and the American Philosophical Society," the letter stated, "and inasmuch as a reproduction of the gavel could in no way be considered a commercial venture, we consider the request most appropriate." Permission was promptly granted and appropriate arrange-

---

[73] Communication to the writer from the late Julian P. Boyd, June 13, 1974.
[74] Communications to the writer from the late Julian P. Boyd, May 28, 1975, June 28, 1974.

ments were made to enable examination of the original and measurements and description taken.[75]

At first it was proposed to have a replica turned in wood of a large branch broken in a 1973 storm from a copper beech that had been planted at Monticello by Jefferson. Subsequently it was decided to have the replica made in solid ivory to duplicate the form and appearance of the original.[76]

The case in which the original is maintained is a replica of Benjamin Franklin's stencil box, the original of which is in the Society's collection, fashioned from the wood of Jefferson's purple beech, and the same wood was used also to make an anvil upon which the knocker was to be used. The box's locking mechanism is a reproduction of an eighteenth century friction lock. An account of the circumstances leading to the production of the replica was engraved upon a silver plaque enclosed within the cover:

> By special permission, this replica of the first gavel of *The Senate of the United States* was made for use by officers of *The American Philosophical Society*. On this historic square, according to tradition, *Thomas Jefferson* wielded the original while serving simultaneously as president of the Senate and of the Society. This replica rests in a box made from a piece of the still-standing copper beech which he planted in 1807.
>
> Presented to *the American Philosophical Society* on April 13, 1976
> Anniversary of the birth of
> the Author of THE DECLARATION OF INDEPENDENCE

---

[75] Letter signed by Senator Mike Mansfield and Senator Hugh Scott to Hon. William H. Wannall, Sergeant at Arms of the U.S. Senate, April 30, 1975; letters to Mansfield and Scott from Wannall May 6, 1975; letter from Hugh Scott to Julian P. Boyd, May 8, 1975.

[76] Communications from the late Julian P. Boyd to the writer, July 24 and August 6, 1974, May 16 and July 31, 1975, September 20 and December 28, 1976, January 10, 1977.

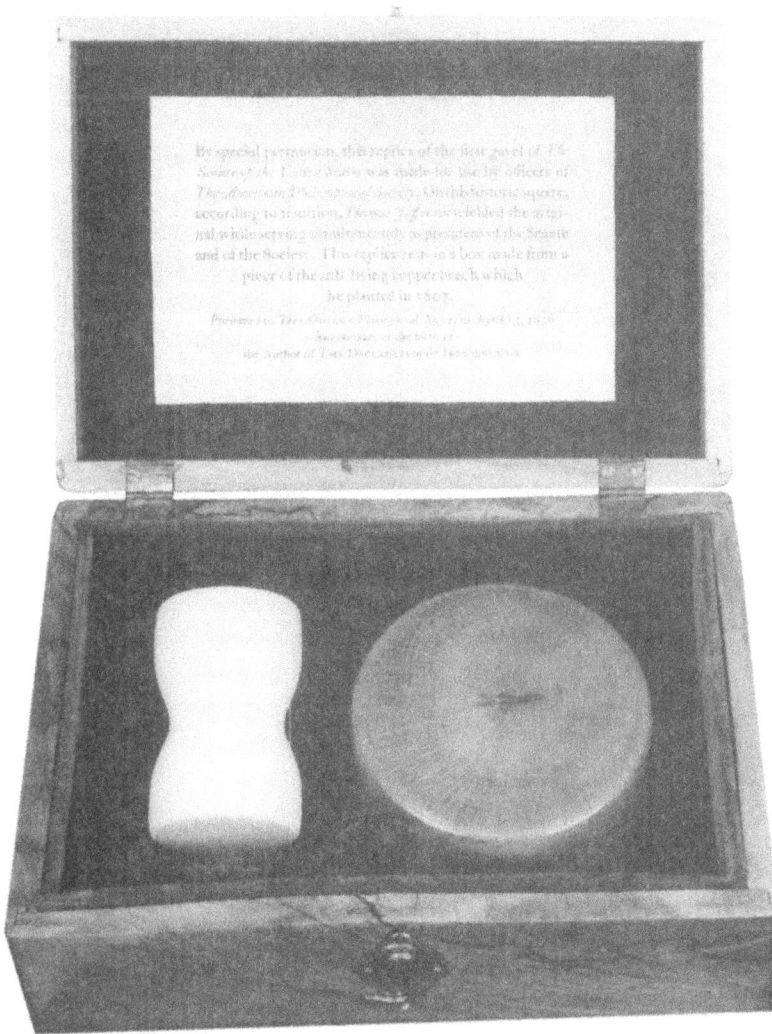

FIGURE 37
The gavel of the American Philosophical Society
based upon the ivory gavel of the United States Senate.

BIBLIOGRAPHY

Manuscripts

OFFICE OF THE ARCHITECT OF THE CAPITOL
  Captain Isaac Bassett, *Reminiscences*

THE LIBRARY OF CONGRESS
  The Papers of Thomas Jefferson
  The Papers of George Washington

NATIONAL ARCHIVES AND RECORDS ADMINISTRATION
  Department of State, *Record Group 59*
  Office of the Secretary of the Treasury, *General Correspondence*
  Department of the Treasury, *Records of the Accounting Officers*
  Papers of the Continental Congress, 34 vols. *Record Group 360* (vol. II)
    File 90, 791, Document 19

SMITHSONIAN INSTITUTION
  Conservation Analytical Laboratory, *Report CAL 1817* (1974)

UNITED STATES SENATE, OFFICE OF THE CURATOR
  Isaac Bassett Papers
  Report of the Secretary of the Senate, 1952

VIRGINIA STATE ARCHIVES
  Papers of Henry Lee
  Papers of William Tatham
  Papers of William Thornton

VIRGINIA STATE LIBRARY
  Executive Letter Book, 1792–1794
  Journals of the House of Burgesses (6 vols.)

Printed Works

ARMSTRONG, WILLIAM. *The Aristocracy of New York: Who They Are and What They Were; Being a Social and Business History of the City For Many Years, by An Old Resident.* New York: New York Publishing Co., 1848.

ARNOLD, HOWARD PAYSON. *Historic Side-Lights.* New York: Harper & Brothers Company, 1899.

BEARD, C. A., ed. *The Journal of William Maclay, United States Senator from Pennsylvania, 1789–1791.* New York: Albert & Charles Boni, 1927.

BEDINI, SILVIO A. *Thinkers and Tinkers. Early American Men of Science.* New York: Charles Scribner's Sons, 1975.

BOYD, JULIAN P., ed. *The Papers of Thomas Jefferson.* 26 vols. Princeton: Princeton University Press, 1950– .

BROCK, R. A. *The Official Records of Robert Dinwiddie, Lieutenant-Governor of the Colony of Virginia, 1751–1758.* Richmond: Virginia Historical Society, 1883.

BROWN, JOAN SAYERS. "William Adams and the Mace of the United States House of Representatives," *Antiques*, vol. CVIII, No. 1, July 1975, pp. 76–77.

———. "A Sterling Saga of Smiths and Silver," *The Washington Post*, January 4, 1976, pp. B16–B17.

———. "The Mace: A Proper Symbol of Office," *The Washington Star*, June 5, 1977, p. 23.

BROWNING, A. R. *The Mace*. Canberra: Australian Government Publishing Service, 1970.

BURNETT, EDMUND C. *Letters of Members of the Continental Congress*. 8 vols. Gloucester, Mass.: 1963.

BUTTERFIELD, LYMAN H., ed. *Diary and Autobiography of John Adams*. 4 vols. Cambridge: Harvard University Press, 1961.

———, et al., eds. *The Book of Abigail and John Adams. Selected Letters of the Adams Family, 1762–1784*. Cambridge, Mass. Harvard University Press, 1975.

BYRD, ROBERT C. *The Senate 1789–1989. Addresses on the History of the United States Senate. Senate Document 100-20*. 4 vols. Washington: U.S. Government Printing Office, 1988.

CARSON, HAMPTON L. "The First Congress of the United States," *The Pennsylvania Magazine of History and Biography*, vol. XIII, No. 2, 1889, pp. 129–52.

COIT, MARGARET L. *John C. Calhoun, American Portrait*. Boston: Houghton Mifflin Co., 1950.

COLEMAN, ELIZABETH DABNEY. "Ceremonial Symbol in Silver," *Virginia Cavalcade*, vol. 5, No. 3.

CROCE, GEORGE C. and DAVID H. WALLACE. *The New-York Historical Society's Dictionary of Artists in America 1564–1860*. New Haven: Yale University Press, 1957.

DAVID, JOHN D. *English Silver at Williamsburg*. Williamsburg: Colonial Williamsburg Foundation, 1966.

DAVIS, POLLY ANN. *Alben B. Barkley Senate Majority Leader and Vice President*. New York: Garland Publishing Co., 1979.

DE PAUW, LINDA GRANT, C. B. BICKFORD and LaVONNE M. SIEGEL, eds. *Documentary History of the First Federal Congress of the United States of America, March 4, 1789–March 3, 1791. Volume I, Senate Legislative Journal*. 2 vols. Baltimore: The Johns Hopkins University Press, 1972.

Dictionary of American Biography, edited by Allen Johnson, et al., 20 vols. and Supplements. New York: Charles Scribner's Sons, 1928–36, 1944–95.

DONALD, DAVID. *Charles Sumner and the Coming of the Civil War*. New York: Alfred A. Knopf, 1960).

ELLIOT, JONATHAN. *The Debates in the Several State Conventions on the Adoption of the Federal Constitution*. 4 vols. New York: 1836.

The Encyclopedia Britannica. A Dictionary of Arts, Sciences, Literature and General Information. 11th edition, 29 vols. New York: The Encyclopedia Britannica Company, 1911.

Encyclopedia Britannica. 24 vols. Chicago: Encyclopedia Britannica, Inc., 1943.

FEINSILBER, MICHAEL. "Righting Independence Time," *The Washington Post*, November 12, 1976. p. B8.

FORD, PAUL LEICESTER, ed. *The Writings of Thomas Jefferson.* 10 vols. New York: G. P. Putnam's Sons, 1895– .

FORD, WORTHINGTON CHAUNCEY et al., *Journals of the Continental Congress, 1774–1789.* 34 vols. Washington: The Library of Congress, 1904–7.

GERRY, ROGER G. "Richard Patten: Mathematical Instrument Maker," *Antiques*, July 1969.

GOODWIN, RUTHERFORD. *A Brief & True Report Concerning Williamsburg in Virginia* . . . Williamsburg: Colonial Williamsburg, Inc. 1959.

"The Hall of Representatives, Washington," *The Illustrated London News*, April 6, 1861, p. 320.

HARDING, KENNETH S. *The Mace. A History of the Mace and Its Use in the House of Representatives of the United States.* Washington: Government Printing Office, 1972.

HARVEY, SIR PAUL, ed. *The Oxford Companion to English Literature.* New York/Oxford: Oxford University Press, 1940.

HATSELL, JOHN. *Precedents of Proceedings in the House of Commons.* 2 vols. London: 1878.

HAYNES, GEORGE H. *The Senate of the United States. Its History and Practice.* 2 vols. Boston: Houghton Mifflin Company, 1938.

HEISER, DAVID C. R. *South Carolina's Mace and Its Heritage.* Columbia, S.C.: South Carolina House of Representatives, 1991.

HINDS, ASHER C. *Hinds' Precedents of the House of Representatives of the United States.* 2 vols. ? Washington: Government Printing Office, 1907.

HONAN, WILLIAM H. "Mr. President, Distinguished Colleagues . . . (The Art of Oratory In the Senate of the United States)," *Esquire Magazine*, May 1969, p. 162.

HOOD, GRAHAM. *American Silver. A History of Style, 1650–1900.* New York: Praeger Publishers, 1971.

HOWARD, THOMAS W. "Peter G. Van Winkle's Vote in the Impeachment of Andrew Johnson: A West Virginian As a Profile of Courage," *West Virginia History*, July 1974.

Journal of the First Session of the Senate of the United States of America, Begun and Held at the City of New York, March 4, 1789 . . . Washington: Gales & Seaton, 1820.

Journal of the House of Burgesses. 6 vols. Richmond, Va.: Virginia State Library, 1905–6.

The Mace of the House of Representatives of the United States. Washington, Government Printing Office, 1991. (Commemorative booklet.)

"The Mace of the Virginia House of Burgesses," *Virginia Magazine of History and Biography*, vol. XIX, July 1911, pp. 305–6.

[MADISON, JAMES]. *Notes of Debates in the Federal Convention of 1787 Reported by James Madison.* Athens, Ohio: 1984.

MALONE, DUMAS. *Jefferson and His Time. Volume I. Jefferson the Virginian.* Boston: Little, Brown and Company, 1948.

MARBUT, F. B. *News From the Capital. The Story of Washington Reporting.* Carbondale, Ill.: 1971.

MASTERSON, WILLIAM H. *William Blount.* Baton Rouge: 1954.

MCKINNEY, SANDRA, ed. *The South Carolina Legislative Journal.* Columbia, S.C.: N.P., 1990.

The National Intelligencer, September 5, 1811.

Norfolk's Historical Mace. Norfolk, Va.: Virginia National Bank, 1935.

Norfolk's Historic Mace. Norfolk: By Order of the City Council, N.D.

"Norfolk's Historic Mace," *Arts in Virginia*, vol. 1, No. 2, Winter 1961.

ORANGE, SYLVIA W., ed. *South Carolina State Symbols and Emblems.* Excerpted from the *South Carolina Legislative Manual.* Columbia, S.C.: N.P., 1990. "The Mace."

Our Capitol. Senate Document 50. Washington: Government Printing Office, 1966.

The Oxford English Dictionary. 2nd edition. 20 vols. Oxford: Clarendon Press, 1989.

PALMER, WILLIAM PITT, et al., eds. *Calendar of Virginia State Papers and Other Manuscripts . . . Preserved . . . at Richmond (1652–1869).* 11 vols. Richmond: 1875–93.

PAPENFUSE, EDWARD C. "The Speaker's Medallion," address to the Maryland House of Delegates, March 22, 1995.

PARGELLIS, S. M. "The Procedure of the Virginia House of Burgesses," *William and Mary College Quarterly Historical Magazine*, Second Series, vol. VII, No. 2, April 1927, pp. 76–77, vol. VII No. 3, July 1927, p. 153.

"Peace Declared in Williamsburg, 1783," *William and Mary College Historical Magazine*, vol. XIV, 1906, pp. 278–79.

PECK, HARRY T., ed. *Harper's Dictionary of Classical Literature and Antiquities.* New York/Chicago: American Book Company, 1896. s.v. "mace."

POORE, BENJAMIN PERLEY. *Reminiscences of Sixty Years in the National Metropolis.* 2 vols. Philadelphia: Hubbard Brothers, 1886.

POWELL, WILLIAM S. *The Correspondence of William Tryon and Other Selected Papers.* Raleigh: Division of Archives and History, Department of Cultural Resources, 1980. Vol. I, p. 448.

REES, ABRAHAM. *The Cyclopaedia, or Universal Dictionary of Arts, Sciences, and Literature.* 39 vols. London: For Longman, Hurst, Rees, Orme, & Brown, 1819.

RIEDEL, RICHARD LANGHAM. *Halls of the Mighty.* Washington: Robert B. Luce, Inc., 1969.

RILEY, ELIHU S. *A History of the General Assembly of Maryland 1635–1904.* Baltimore: 1905.

ROSENBAUM, JEANETTE W. "Myer Myers, early New York goldsmith," *Antiques,* February 1954, pp. 124–27, 154.

RUBICAM, MILTON. "A Memorial of the Life of William Barton, A. M. (1754–1817)," *Pennsylvania History,* vol. XII, July 1945, pp. 179–93.

SALLEY, ALEXANDER SAMUEL. *The Mace.* Historical Commission of South Carolina Bulletin No. 3.

SAUNDERS, WILLIAM L., ed. *The Colonial Records of North Carolina.* Raleigh: Josephus Daniels, 1887. Vol. V, p. 714.

Senate, Report of the Secretary of the, for 1952, p. 292.

"Senate Data," *The Washington Daily News,* September 3, 1960.

Senate Journal, May 21, 1826, p. 402.

"The Senatorial Gavel," *The Washington Post,* 1889.

SMART, CHARLES E. *The Makers of Surveying Instruments in America Since 1700.* Troy, N.Y.: Regal Art Press, 1962.

SMITH, ELBERT B. *Magnificent Missourian, Thomas Hart Benton.* Philadelphia: 1905.

[SMITH, JOHN COTTON]. ANDREWS, REV. WILLIAM W., ed., *The Correspondence and Miscellanies of the Hon. John Cotton Smith.* New York: Harper and Brothers, 1847.

U.S. Congress. *Congressional Globe,* 27th Congress, 2nd session, p. 71; 31st Congress, 1st session, p. 27; 35th Congress, 1st session, p. 603; 42nd Congress, 2nd session, April 20, 1872, pp. 2627, 2629; 1st Congress, 1st session, February 24, 1879, pp. 1844–48; 13th Congress, 3rd session, February 8, 1815, p. 3276.

U.S. Congress. *Congressional Record,* Washington: 1874– . 46th Congress, 3rd session, p. 311; 48th Congress, 2nd session, pp. 1419–20; 61st Congress, 3rd session, pp. 3235, 4330–31.

U.S. Congress. [*Annals of Congress*]. *Debates and Proceedings in the Congress of the United States 1789–1824.* 42 vols. Washington: 1854–56. 5th Congress, 1st session, May 15, 1797–July 10, 1797; 8th Congress, 2nd session, November 5, 1804–March 3, 1805.

U.S. Congress, Senate. *Journal of the First Session of the Senate of the United States of America Begun and Held at the City of New York, March 4, 1789* . . . . Washington, p. 186.

[Virginia] *Colonial Entry Book.* No. 105, pp. 298–301; *Virginia Historical Magazine*, p. 186.

WALSH, WILLIAM S. *A Handy Book of Curious Information.* Philadelphia: J. B. Lippincott Company, 1913.

WHARTON, FRANCIS, ed., *The Revolutionary Diplomatic Correspondence of the United States.* 6 vols. Washington: Government Printing Office, 1889.

INDEX

84 *Index*